HARDPRESS.NET
HOME OF HARD-TO-FIND BOOKS

Hints for the Improvement of Early Education
and Nursery Discipline
by Mrs. Hoare (Louisa Gurney)

Address:
HardPress
8345 NW 66TH ST #2561
MIAMI FL 33166-2626
USA
Email: info@hardpress.net

E 4

Iam Am

HINTS

FOR THE IMPROVEMENT

OF

EARLY EDUCATION

AND

Nursery Discipline.

"I think I may say, that, of all the men we meet with, nine parts of ten are what they are, good or evil, useful or not, by their education."—LOCKE.

"To neglect beginnings, is the fundamental error into which most parents fall."

"Parents wonder to taste the streams bitter, when they themselves have poisoned the fountain."—LOCKE.

FROM THE TWELFTH LONDON EDITION
WITH ADDITIONS.

NEW-YORK:

WILEY & LONG,

161 Broadway.

1835.

NEW-YORK:

OSBORN AND BUCKINGHAM, PRINTERS, 29 ANN-STREET.

52,823 4/4/92

DEDICATED

TO MOTHERS,

BY

A MOTHER.

CONTENTS.

H I N T S,

&c.

INTRODUCTION.

IT is with considerable diffidence, that the Writer offers to the attention of Mothers, and those engaged in the care and instruction of young children, the following Remarks; though she hopes that their being the simple result of experience, will compensate for their imperfections.

The origin of this little work was as follows: The Author having formed a few rules, as directions for her nursemaid, in the management of her first child, committed them to paper, that they might be the more clearly understood and remembered; and as she

1

found these written rules beneficial in her own nursery, she conceived they might prove useful to others. Whilst attempting, however, to improve and enlarge them, she was persuaded they touched upon so many important points, they were so closely interwoven with the first principles of education, that they could not, with propriety, be addressed to those whose duty is more to *obey* than to *rule ;* and that they were most likely to be useful, as an assistance to a mother, in the exercise of her own authority ; in training those who are to act under her ; and in establishing the discipline of her nursery. Nor was it considered incompatible with such an object to retain the one chapter which treats exclusively of " the motives that should influence a nurse ;" but this being in some measure unconnected with the rest of the work, is placed in the Appendix.

Those " are the golden hours of

childhood," which are spent in the society of a good mother; and it is evident, that a mother cannot do full justice to her family, unless a considerable portion of her time be devoted to it. But, in the various engagements and duties of life, her children cannot be her exclusive object; and, as an injurious influence, though but casually exerted, may counteract the effects of continued care, it is of no small importance that those, to whom she confides them, *whatever be their office*, should be fitted, as far as they are capable of it, to supply her place during her absence. They should therefore be chosen with caution and discretion, instructed in that part of education which devolves upon them, and their defects, as far as possible, remedied.

Good education must be the result of one consistent and connected system; and both the nursery and school-room will become scenes of insubordination or sources of disappointment, if authority be opposed to authority, and influence counteract influence. A judicious mother will, therefore, keep the reins in her own hands; she will be the only source of power; and her assistants should exercise authority, *whether more or less*, simply as derived from her, and in subjection to her. If, at any time, they assume a power which does not belong to them, if they take more than is given, they outstep the bounds of duty, and, in that proportion, diminish their value to the parent, and their usefulness to the children. On the other hand, an assistant should receive the unvarying support and sanction of a mother whilst acting within the prescribed limits, and exercising that portion of authority which has been confided to her. To lay down these limits—to determine what should be this portion, requires an exercise of discretion on the part of the mother. It must depend upon the situation and character of those to whom she intrusts her children, and upon her own individual circumstances.

The principles touched upon in the following Remarks may be applied to education in general; although they are brought forward with a more *particular* reference to the earlier periods of childhood. It is probable that education may be begun sooner than is generally supposed. The sympathies, even of infants, are quick, and powerfully affected by the manner, looks, and tones of voice of those about them. Something, therefore, may undoubtedly be done towards influencing the mind in the first two or three years of infancy; but this will be effected more by avoiding what is hurtful, as irritation or alarm, than by aiming at premature excellence. The minds of children, as their bodies, are not to be forced. We are to follow the leadings of nature—" to go her pace "—to be ever watchful, diligent and alert, to make the best use of the opportunities and advantages which she throws in our way : for it is to be remembered, that nature may be cramped and forced, rather than corrected and improved ; and that, in every doubtful case, it is wise to incline to the lenient, rather than to the severe side of the question ; because an excess of freedom is safer than too much restraint.

GENERAL PRINCIPLES OF EDUCATION.

SUCCESS in Education depends,

FIRST—*More on Prevention than Cure;* more on securing our children from injury, than on forcing upon them what is right. If we wish, for instance, to render a child courageous, we shall effect it, not so much by urging and compelling them to feats of hardihood, as by guarding him from all impressions of terror, or from witnessing a weak and cowardly spirit in others.

SECONDLY,—*On Example rather than on Precept and Advice.*

As the bodies of children are imperceptibly affected by the air they breathe, so are their minds by the moral atmosphere which surrounds them; that is, the tone of character and general influence of those with whom they live.

THIRDLY,—*On forming Habits rather than on inculcating rules.*

It is little to tell a child what to do, we must show him how to do it, and see that it is done.   It is nothing to enact laws, if we do not take care that they are put into practice, and adopted as habits.   This is the chief business of education, and the most neglected ; for it is more easy to command, than to teach and enforce.   For example; a child will never know how to write by a set of rules, however complete ; the pen must be put into his hand, and the power acquired by repeated efforts, and continued practice.

FOURTHLY—*On regulating our Conduct, with reference to the Formation of the Character when matured, rather*

*than by confining our Views to the im-
mediate effect of our labour.*

Premature acquirements, premature
quickness of mind, premature feeling,
and even premature propriety of conduct, are not often the evidences of real
strength of character, and are rarely
followed by corresponding fruits in future life.

LASTLY,—*On bearing in mind a just
sense of the Comparative Importance
of the objects at which we aim.*

As in the general conduct of life, it
is the part of wisdom to sacrifice the
less to the greater good, so is this
eminently the case in the subject before
us. Now the primary, the essential
object of education is this,—to form in
children a religious habit of mind,
founded on the divine principles of
Christianity, and leading to the habitual
exercise of practical virtue. To this,

all other attainments are wholly sub-
ordinate.

These points, though frequently referred to in the following Observations,
are thus stated separately, that they
may be the more easily kept in view,
as fundamental principles of universal
application, in executing the particular
directions that follow.

TRUTH AND SINCERITY.

NOTHING, perhaps, is more beautiful,
or more rare, than a character in
which is no guile. Guile insinuates
itself into our hearts and conduct, to a
degree of which we are little aware.
Many who would be shocked at an
actual breach of truth, are, notwithstanding, far from sincere in manner
or conversation. The mode in which
they speak of others, when absent, is
wholly inconsistent with their pro-
fessions to them, when present. They
will relate a fact, not falsely, but
leaning to that side which tells best
for themselves ; they represent their
own actions in the fairest colours ;
they have an excuse ever ready for

themselves, and too often at the expense of others. Such conduct, if not coming under the character of direct falsehood, is certainly a species of deceit to be severely condemned, and strictly guarded against, not only in ourselves, but in our children; for we shall find them early prone to art, and quick in imbibing it from others. It is not enough, therefore, to speak the truth; our whole behaviour to them should be sincere, upright, fair, and without artifice; and it is experience alone that can prove the excellent effects that will result from such a course of conduct. Let all who are engaged in the care of children consider it a duty of primary, of essential importance, never to deceive them, never to employ cunning to gain their ends, or to spare present trouble. Let them not, for instance, to prevent a fit of crying, excite expectation of a pleasure which they are not certain can be procured; or assure a child that the medicine he must take is nice, when they know to the contrary. If a question be asked them, which they are unwilling or unable to answer, let them freely confess it, and let them not be ashamed to make this confession: for children often ask questions which puzzle wise heads in making answers; but always beware of assuming power or knowledge which they do not possess; for all artifice is not only sinful, but is generally detected, even by children: and we shall experience the truth of the old proverb, " a cunning trick helps but once, and hinders ever after." No one who is not experimentally acquainted with children, would conceive how clearly they distinguish betwen truth and artifice; or how readily they adopt those equivocal expedients in their own behalf, which they perceive, are practised against them.

Great caution is required in making
2

promises, and in threatening punishment; but we must be rigid in the
performance of the one, and in the
infliction of the other. If, for example we assure a child unconditionally,
that after his lessons he shall have a
top or a ball, no subsequent ill-beha-
viour on his part should induce us to
deprive him of it. Naughty or good
the top must be his; and if it be necessary to punish him, we must do it in
some other way than by breach of en-
gagement. *For our word, once passed,
must not be broken.*

We should labour to excite in children a detestation of all that is mean,
cunning, or false; to inspire them with
a spirit of openness, honour, and perfect honesty; making them feel how
noble it is, not merely to speak the
truth, but to speak the simple unaltered
truth, whether it tell for or against
themselves; but this we cannot effect,
unless our example uniformly concur

with our instructions. We should
teach them not only to confess their
faults, but to confess them freely, and
entirely, without prefacing them by excuses, or endeavouring to lessen their
own offence, by laying blame upon
another. When referring to others
their mutual complaints and disputes,
they should be warned to relate the case
honourably and fairly, to state both
sides of the question—to be willing to
accuse themselves as well as their companions. In these points even conscientious children, who dread a falsehood, are extremely prone to equivo-
cate, and to keep back, at least, part of
the truth. The habit of idle gossip-
ping, of seeking and dispensing amusement, by hearing and repeating the
affairs of others, is one great source of
misrepresentation, and not unfrequently
even of direct falsehood. The dawnings of such a habit are to be checked,
the meanness of tale-bearing and de-

traction must be strongly impressed upon the mind in early life, and children reminded that not only duty, but a sense of honour should lead us to speak of others in absence as we would do in their presence.

The confusion and undesigned inaccuracy, so often to be observed in conversation, especially in that of uneducated persons, proves that " truth needs to be cultivated as a talent as well as a virtue," children require not only to be *told* to speak the truth, but *taught* how to do it. To this end, it will be highly beneficial to accustom them gradually and by continued practice, to give an accurate account of what they have read or seen, and to relate correctly circumstances in which they have themselves been engaged; for this perspicuity and precision are commonly the result not only of good principle but of intellectual cultivation. Dr. Johnson observes, " Nothing but experience can evince the frequency of false information; some men relate what they think as what they know; some men of confused memories and habitual inaccuracy ascribe to one man what belongs to another, and some talk on without thought or care. Accustom your children, therefore, to a strict attention to truth, even in the most minute particulars: if a thing happened at one window, and they, when relating it, say that it happened at another, do not let it pass, but instantly check them; you do not know where deviation from truth will end. IT IS MORE FROM CARELESSNESS ABOUT TRUTH, THAN FROM INTENTIONAL LYING, THAT THERE IS SO MUCH FALSEHOOD IN THE WORLD."*

On no account whatever let any

* See Boswell's Life of Johnson, octavo, vol. iii. pp. 249, 250.

2*

thing be said or done in the nursery,
that Mamma is not to be told.

In case of any unpleasant occur-
rence, it is the duty of a nurse to take
the earliest opportunity of informing
her mistress; and to do this when she
can with propriety, in the presence of
the children. She is ever to enforce
the same habit among them, encouraging them, if they have met with an
accident, or committed a fault, at once,
(for, in these cases, delays are dangerous,) to go to their mother, and
freely to confess it to her.

It is desirable, as far as possible, to
manifest confidence in the honour and
veracity of children; for we should
wish deceit and falsehood to be considered among them as offences of
which we do not even suppose them
capable; to accuse a child falsely,
breaks his spirit, and lowers his sense
of honour. If we have, at any time,

reason to suspect a child of telling a
falsehood, or of concealing the truth,
great caution is necessary in betraying
that suspicion.   We should endeavour
to ascertain the fact by our own observation, or the evidence of others,
rather than by the common expedient of
questioning the child himself, or strongly
urging him to confession; for, in so
doing, we shall often lead him, if he be
guilty, to repeat the falsehood; or, if
innocent and timid, to plead guilty to
a fault which he has not committed.
Besides, no small care is necessary that
we do not bring children into temptation, or put too much to the proof, their
still weak and unformed principles.
There are many suspicious cases, the
truth of which being buried in the
breast of a child, cannot be discovered;
and these it is generally wiser to leave
unnoticed; at the same time more vigi-
lantly observing the offender, and treating him with the greater strictness upon

those occasions in which the truth can be ascertained by positive evidence. For example; were a child to assure me that he had so many times read over his lesson to himself, and I had reason to doubt the fact, I would let it pass in silence, dreading the effects of ill-placed suspicion, and knowing, that, if he were guilty and should choose to deny it, I had no means by which to convict him. On the other hand, if a child tell a nurse that his mother has desired she should give him fruit, or a cake, and she suspect he is deceiving her, let her say nothing to him at the time, but apply, without his knowledge, to the mother; should her suspicions be confirmed, the child is convicted, and the opportunity is at once afforded for reproving and correcting him with decision; and, indeed, unless we are *morally certain* that a child is guilty of falsehood, we should never accuse it of so doing, even by the slightest insinuation.

If we have grounds for supposing a child guilty of some common offence, although, as has before been remarked with regard to falsehood, it is better to ascertain the truth by evidence, rather than by the forced confession of the suspected party; yet, sometimes, it may be necessary to question the child himself. This must be done with great caution, not with the vehemence and hurry so commonly employed on such occasions; but with calmness and affection. We should forbid him to answer in haste, or without consideration, reminding him of the extreme importance and happy consequences of truth, of our tenderness towards him, and willingness to forgive, if he freely confess his fault, and show himself upright and honourable in his conduct; for truth being the corner-stone of practical goodness, we must be ready, when necessary, to sacrifice to it less important points; and, for the sake of this leading object, to pass over many smaller offences.

I cannot close the subject before us, without a warning against a severe, repulsive, disheartening, or satirical system in the management of children. Nothing is so likely to produce in them, especially in those of timid dispositions, reserve, pusillanimity, and duplicity of character. On the other hand, good discipline will greatly promote habits of integrity and openness. But it is to be remembered, that the *best discipline* is always combined with freedom, mildness, sympathy, and affection. Never rule your children by fear; for in so doing you make them *slaves*, and not *sons and daughters*.

AUTHORITY AND OBEDIENCE.

ALL who are engaged in bringing up children must, necessarily, possess a certain share of authority or power over them. This power, being the chief instrument in education, it is to the injudicious use which is made of it, that many of the prevalent defects amongst children are to be ascribed. ———On the one hand, we may observe self-indulgence, insubordination, and disobedience; on the other, a broken and depressed spirit, one of the most serious, and least curable evils which ill-management, on the part of those who govern, can occasion. The former, arising from a weak, indecisive, and irregular exercise of authority; the latter, from coldness and severity.

It is our business to steer as clear as possible between these opposite evils—bearing in mind that it is essential to the welfare of children to know how to obey, to submit their wills, and to bear a denial; while, at the same time, their minds should be left free and vigorous, open to every innocent enjoyment, and unfettered by the thraldom of fear. We shall best unite these important advantages by an authority firm, but affectionate, equally free from peevishness or ill-temper, and an excess of indulgence, regular and consistent, never unnecessarily called into action, but always with effect; exercised with a simple view to the good of those under our care, according to the dictates of judgment, and from the principle of love; for the reproofs, corrections, and restraints, which are necessarily imposed upon children should spring from love, as well as the encourage-

ments and indulgences which we bestow
upon them ;——

———" Such authority, in show,
When most severe and must'ring all its force,
Is but the graver countenance of love,
Whose favour, like the clouds of spring may low'r,
And utter, now and then, an awful voice,
But has a blessing in its darkest frown,
Threat'ning at once and nourishing the plant."

Authority thus guarded, combining
in right proportion, decision and mildness, will produce, in the subjects of
it, an invaluable union of happy freedom and ready obedience.

Decision of character is essential to
success in the business of education.
" Weakness in every form tempts ar-
rogance ; when a firm decisive spirit is
recognised, it is curious to see how the
space clears around a man, and leaves
him room and freedom. I have known
several parents, both fathers and mothers, whose management of their families has answered this description,

3

and has displayed a striking example of the facile complacency with which a number of persons of different ages and dispositions will yield to the decisions of a firm mind, *acting on an equitable and enlightened system.*" * But while we do justice to this great and most effectual quality, it must never be forgotten that decision, when untempered by affection, and unpoised by a wise, considerate, generous estimate of the rights of others, too quickly degenerates into sternness and severity.

And is not authority often converted into an instrument of evil rather than of good, by being exerted for self-gratification, from temper, from impulse, and sometimes from that love of rule which closely borders upon tyranny?

What is more common, too, than a frequent, weak, irritating exercise of

* Foster's Essay on Decision of Character.

power, which teazes the child, and frets his temper, whilst it rarely commands his obedience?

A nurse forbids a child to meddle with the pen and ink with which he is playing, but he goes on, as if deaf to her voice. She repeats her prohibition in a louder and more peevish tone, " Don't do so, I will tell your papa; I shall punish you if you go on." The child obeys perhaps for a minute; but having often heard the like threats, and as rarely found them executed, he soon creeps to the table, and again lays hold of the forbidden objects.

The nurse complains how unmanageable are her children, little supposing that she herself is the cause!

She should, in the first instance, with kindness and decision, have told the child that she forbad his playing with ink and pens, and therefore, that it must not be done. Should more be necessary, let her add that, in case of his once again transgressing, she shall be obliged to send him out of the room, or to take him to his papa.

The *absolute* necessity of executing these threats, has already been remarked.

When the child sees his attendant rise to do it, he will very often, *then*, relent, and *then* submit, promising to repeat his offence no more; but this should make no difference; it would be merely adding to future trouble, and to future disobedience—*Our word once passed, must not be broken.*

Also, if a child be fretting or crying, it will little avail to say that he is naughty, and to order him many times, to be still. Rather let him be told that, if in five minutes (for we should allow him time to recover himself) he is not perfectly quiet, he must be removed from the table, or sent into the next room.

In such cases, it is of comparatively little use to threaten punishment, generally—we should always state the particular privation which we mean to impose.

It is the result of experience, that authority is to be established rather by *actions* than *words*. What is vulgarly called *scolding*, is altogether unnecessary; the government of the tongue is therefore essential to those engaged in the business of education. In *mind* and *action* we should be firm; in *manner* mild and quiet. It is a common mistake to talk too much, to make too much noise in managing children—a multiplicity of words—complaints—encouragements—rebukes—threats—but nothing done, nothing effected, when probably one decided action would have accomplished the object without further trouble.

For example; a child gives way to temper and passionate crying at his

3*

morning dressing; the nurse prolongs
the evil, and adds to the noise by
her upbraidings and persuasions, which
at the moment of irritation, of course
avail nothing. She had better be silent
at the time, calmly pursuing her usual
course, and at breakfast, should her
mistress approve it, the offender may
be deprived of some little indulgence
which the other children are enjoying.
Only let her take care to do this with
kindness, explaining the reason of her
conduct, but not upbraiding him with
his fault; assuring him of the pain it
gives her to deprive him of any gratification, and of the pleasure she will feel
in bestowing the same upon him when
his behaviour shall deserve it. This
mode of proceeding will effect more
than an abundant repetition of mere
admonitions and rebukes.

I would never reward a child for
doing *duty*, for thereby you lower the
standard of *moral duty*. Punish it if it

acts wrong; but if it acts well, let it look for its reward from some higher source than myself. In other words, let it learn to perform a duty because the *will of God and the will of the parent* both required it; not because I reward it.

With children, a vigilant superintendence is required, but not a frequent interference.

The object of education " is to preserve them from evil, not from childishness."

We should therefore be very lenient to those errors, which are more " the defects of the *age* than of the individual," and which time, there is little doubt, will remove, reserving our authority to be exercised with the more effect on important occasions—such occasions as bear upon fundamental principles and moral habits.

Children must, and should be children still, and it is our duty to sympathize with them as such; to impose upon them no unnecessary restraint, to grant them every harmless gratification, and, as far as possible, to promote their truest enjoyment, remembering that, although the day is often cloudy, yet it is mercifully ordered that the dawn of life should be bright and happy, unless by mismanagement it be rendered otherwise.

It may, at first sight, appear inconsistent with what has been just said, strongly to recommend that the will be effectually subjected in very early childhood. This object must be obtained, if we would proceed in the business of education with comfort, or insure the welfare and happiness of our children. A portion of stricter discipline may, for a time, be required; but discipline, let it ever be remembered, is perfectly compatible with the tenderest sympathy and the most affectionate kindness. Many persons, who allow themselves to treat children, during their earliest years, merely as playthings, humouring their caprices, and sacrificing to present fancies their future welfare, when the charm of infancy is past, commence a system of restraint and severity, and betray displeasure and irritability at the very defects of which they have themselves laid the foundation. But if authority has been thoroughly established in the beginning of life, we shall have it the more in our power to grant liberty and indulgence, and to exercise a genial influence over our children, when their feelings are ripening, and when their affection and confidence towards their parents are of increasing importance. Amidst the various objects of education, the cultivation of *confidential* habits is too-often overlooked, even by affectionate and attentive parents. They are, perhaps, obeyed, respected, and beloved; but this is not sufficient. If, in addition, a parent can be to her children the familiar friend, the unreserved confidant, the sympathizing partner in their joys and sorrows, hopes and disappointments, a hold on the mind is obtained, which will continue when authority ceases, and will prove a safeguard through the most critical period of life.

It is important, in the management of children, to make but few rules, and to be unalterably firm in enforcing those which are made : to give no needless commands, but to see that those given are strictly obeyed. We should also be cautious of employing authority on occasions in which it is likely to be exerted in vain, or of commanding what we cannot enforce. If, for example, we desire a child to bring a book, and he refuse, we can clasp the book in his hand, and oblige him to deliver it. But if we have imprudently declared that he shall not dine or walk till he has repeated a poem, or spoken a particular sentence, should he choose to resist, we cannot compel him; and this affords an obstinate child the opportunity for obtaining a victory over those to whom he ought to submit.

There are cases in which children, without any ill intention, are unable to obey; and in these, also, they should not be commanded. Of this, personal tricks are an example :—" My dear, don't bite your nails," may be repeated a dozen times in the course of a lesson; but such is the force of habit, that the hand still involuntarily finds its way to the mouth. If we are determined to overcome the propensity, it must be done by some external restraint, as by fastening the hand in a glove, &c.; *not* by commands, which, as they cannot be obeyed, serve only to impair the habit of ready obedience.

It is the part of wisdom, as far as possible, so to exercise authority, that it should be considered as inviolable, never to be disobeyed or contemned with impunity.

The restraint of the tongue, which has before been mentioned as necessary to those who educate, is one of the most important habits to be enforced also upon children themselves, and is a great security to proper submission under authority; forming no small part of that self-subjection which is essential to true discipline. Impertinent and disrespectful language is not to be allowed; for, this once admitted, it is the certain harbinger of actual insub-ordination, and a train of other evils.

REWARDS AND PUNISHMENTS, PRAISE AND BLAME.

REWARDS and punishments, praise and blame, are the main supports of authority, and its effect will greatly depend on our dispensing these with wisdom and caution.

A very frequent recourse to rewards does but lessen their effect, and weaken the mind by accustoming it to an unnecessary and improper stimulus, whilst punishment too freely administered will fret the temper, or, which is worse, break the spirit.

Locke remarks, "that those children who are the most chastised rarely prove the best men; and that punishment, if it be not productive of good, will certainly be the cause of much injury."

4

It is better, therefore, if possible, to effect our purpose by encouragement and rewards, rather than correction. But if this be impracticable, we should still keep in view that punishment, being in itself an evil, and intended simply to deter from what is wrong, and to induce submission and penitence, ought never to be extended beyond what is absolutely necessary to secure these objects, and, unless inflicted by parents, or those who are possessed of the first authority, should be of the mildest and least alarming character.

Not only the rod, but severe reproaches, rough handling, tying to bedposts, the hasty slap, the dark closet, and every thing that might terrify the imagination, are to be excluded from the nursery. If a nurse be under the necessity of punishing a child, she may confine him for a time in a light room, remove him from table, or allow him

simply to suffer the natural consequences of his offence. If he inten-
tionally hurt his brother with a whip,
the whip must for a time be taken from
him. If he betray impatience and selfishness at table, let him be served the
last, and with the least indulgence.
Such gentle measures, administered
with decision, will generally succeed;
for it is much more *the certainty and
immediate execution*, than the *severity*
of punishment, that will avail. A child,
who is sure of being confined a quarter of an hour if he strikes his companion, is less likely to commit the
offence than another who has only the
apprehension that he *may* be detained
an hour; for the hope of escaping
with impunity, adds no little force to
temptation. Correction, also, is not
to be unnecessarily delayed or prolonged. Delay renders it less effectual, and more trying to the temper;
whilst any needless continuance, in

every way increases the evils, and
lessens the benefits which might result from it.

There is much in education to be
done by watching our opportunities,
by acting at the right season. With
most children there is an era, and
this often takes place as they are
emerging from boyhood, in which a
struggle is made for the mastery,—in
which is to be decided who is to
rule,—the child, or those who are
placed over him. At such a juncture,
in order to determine the matter, and
firmly to establish authority, it will
be necessary to employ vigorous measures, and to suppress the first risings
of a rebellious and disobedient spirit by
punishment, decisive; and repeated till
submission on the part of the child, and
victory on that of the parent are com-
pletely secured.* So great is the im-

* Although the use of the rod is *most strictly* to
be prohibited to those who possess only secondary

portance of these contests, so great the difficulty of carrying them on with the temper, and the union of firmness and affection, which they require, that it is desirable they should be conducted only by a parent. Punishment is more often to be inflicted simply as the *conse-*

authority, yet, with some *few* children, a *parent* may find it necessary to employ corporal punishment in order to establish the habit of obedience, or effectually to subdue a propensity to falsehood, or to any other glaring breach of moral principle. Under such circumstances corporal punishment may be very efficacious ; but to render it so, or rather, to prevent its becoming a *dangerous* evil, it must be resorted to only as a *last* resource on very important occasions, and administered as a chastisement of the most serious nature, with decision, perfect serenity of temper, and affection towards the offender.

It will also be found that corporal punishment, if necessary at all, will be most useful in the early stages of childhood ; every advancing year, as it should add to a child's generosity of feeling and sense of honor, increases the *serious* disadvantages which attend this mode of correction.

4*

quence of a fault, and not with the idea that it must be prolonged till the particular action required has been performed.

A child is desired, for instance, to put up his playthings, and he refuses, with so much self-will, that his attendant cannot overlook it, and is under the necessity of telling him that he must be confined in the next room for a quarter of an hour ; but let her beware of adding, that there he shall stay till he *will* put them up. This would serve merely to engage in the combat his pride and his obstinacy. At the end of the quarter of an hour she should release him from his imprisonment, without waiting to make conditions for his future obedience.

It has been said, indeed, that submission on the part of the offender, is the object of punishment, and such submission as may entitle him to receive complete forgiveness. When a child has been corrected we should not rest satisfied till this object has been attained; but it is not, in all cases, to be expected, either during the continuance of the punishment, or immediately afterwards.

A well-trained child, if affectionately admonished after correction is over, not being irritated at the idea that it may be continued, will generally yield at once: but it is not to be considered necessary to put this always to the proof. He has committed a fault, and has suffered the consequences. Here it is often the wisest to leave the affair for the time, choosing the *earliest* favourable opportunity, when he has more perfectly recovered himself, for receiving his submission, and assuring him of forgiveness.

If his attendant have conducted herself in the right spirit, he will have felt the force of her correction, though he may not have shown it at the time.

The next day, if she desire him to put up his playthings, he will pretty certainly, obey with more than common alacrity.

When a child has been punished, he should be restored as soon as possible to favour; and when he has received forgiveness, treated as if nothing had happened. He may be affectionately reminded of his fault in private, as a warning for the future; but, after peace has been made, to upbraid him with it, especially in the presence of others, is almost a breach of honour, and certainly a great unkindness. Under any circumstances, to reproach children in company is equally useless and painful to them, and is generally done from irritability of temper, with little view to their profit.

We are to remember that *shame* will not effectually deter children from what is wrong; and that in employing it too much as an instrument of education, we have reason to apprehend we may lead them to act from the fear of man, rather than from that of God. Every thing, too, which may in the least injure the characters of children, is to be strictly avoided. To have the *name* of a naughty child will produce so disheartening an effect upon the mind, that the ill consequences may probable be felt through life. It is on this account desirable that tutors, governesses, and nurses, be cautious of enlarging upon the faults of those under their care to any but the parents.

Blame, and even praise, are to be dispensed with nearly as much caution as punishments and rewards; for a child may be called " good," " naughty, " troublesome," " kind," or unkind," till either his temper will be kept in continual irritation, or he will listen with perfect indifference.

A child must not be punished or reproved from the impulse of temper;

we may regulate his actions, but we cannot hope to subdue his will, or improve his disposition, by a display of our own wilfulness and irritability; for our example will more than counteract the good effects of our correction. If irritated, we should wait till we are cool, before we inflict punishment, and then do it as a duty, in exact proportion to the real faultiness of the offender; not to the degree of vexation he has occasioned ourselves. A child should be praised, reproved, rewarded, and corrected, not according, to the *consequences*, but according to the *motives*, of his actions—solely with reference to the right or wrong intention which has influenced him.

Children, therefore, should not be punished for mere accidents, but mildy warned against similar carelessness in future. Whereas some people show much greater displeasure with a child for accidentally overthrowing the table, or breaking a piece of china, than for telling an untruth; or, if he hang his head, and will not show off in company, he is more blamed than for selfishness in the nursery. But does not such treatment arise from preferring our own gratification to the good of the child? and can we hope, by thus doing, to improve him in the government of his temper, or to instruct him in the true standard of right and wrong?

Punishment administered in anger is no longer the discipline of love, but bears too much the character of revenging an injury, and will certainly excite in the sufferer a corresponding temper of mind. From fear, indeed, he may yield externally, but the feelings of his heart would lead him to resentment rather than to penitence and submission. And let it never be forgotten, that if we desire to perform our duties to children, it is not their outward conduct, but to the heart, that we must direct our chief attention.

To punish with effect requires decision, and sometimes courage. If, in addition to this, our punishment scarry with them the stamp of love; if they are inflicted with an undisturbed serenity of temper, with a simple view to the good of the offender, "not for our pleasure, but his profit," they will rarely fail in accomplishing the intended purpose; for children have a quick sense of the motives that influence us, and their hearts are not unfrequently as much softened, and their affections as powerfully called forth, by such corrections, as by the most gratifying rewards that could be bestowed upon them.

TEMPER.

On no part of the character has education more influence, than on the temper; the due regulation of which, is an object of great importance to the enjoyment of the present life, and to the preparation for a better.

An authority, such as has been described, firm, but affectionate; decided, yet mild; imposing no unnecessary restraints; but encouraging every innocent freedom and gratification, exercised according to the dictates of judgment, and supported by rewards and punishments judiciously dispensed, is the best means of securing good temper in our children; and evinces that self-subjection on our part, which is essential to its successful cultivation on theirs. This, at once, will put an end to those impulses of

5

temper in ourselves which are the most
fruitful sources of irritation to others;
for, it is surprising how quickly our
own irritability will be reflected in the
little ones around us. Speak to a child
in a fretful manner, and we shall generally find that his manner partakes of
the same character. We may reprove;
we may punish; we may enforce obedience; but all will be done with double the effect if our own temper remain perfectly unruffled;   for what
benefit can reasonably be expected,
when we recommend that by our injunctions, which we renounce by our
example ?

The variations and inconsistency to
which characters of impulse are also
liable, are particularly trying to children.   There are few tempers that
can resist the effect of being sharply
reproved at one time, for what, at another, is passed over without notice;
of being treated one day with excessive

indulgence, and the next, with fretfulness and severity.

We all have our weak and irritable moments; we may experience many changes of temper and feeling; but let us beware of betraying such variations in our outward conduct, if we value the good temper and respect of our children; for these we have no right to expect on their part, without consistency on ours.

If a fault be glaring, it must be seriously taken up; but in the management of the temper, especially in early childhood, much may be effected by a system of prevention. A judicious attendant may avert many an impending naughty fit, by change of object, gentle amusement, and redoubled care, to put no temptation in the way, if she observe any of her little ones weary, uncomfortable, or irritable. This, for instance, will generally be the case with children when they first awake.

They should therefore then be treated with more than common tenderness; never roused from sleep suddenly or violently; nor exposed to any little trials till they have had time thoroughly to recover themselves. It is scarcely necessary to add, how peculiarly this tender consideration is required, not only in illness, but under the various lesser indispositions so frequent in infancy.

Children ought not to be unnecessarily thwarted in their objects, which, at a very early age, they pursue with eargerness. Let them, if possible, complete their objects without interruption. A child, for example, before he can speak, is trotting after a ball; the nurse snatches him up at the moment, to be washed and dressed, and the poor child throws himself into a violent passion. Whereas had she first entered into his views, kindly assisted him in gaining his object, and then gently taken him up, this trial would have been spared, and his temper uninjured.

We should avoid keeping children in suspense, which is often done from a kind motive, though with a very ill effect. If a child ask his nurse for a cake, and she can give it him, let her tell him so at once, and assure him that he shall have it : but should she be unable to grant his request, or know it would be improper for him, do not let her hesitate ; do not let her say, " I will think of it ; we shall see," but kindly and decidedly refuse him.

If he sees his mother going out, and petition to accompany her, it will be better she should say " No," or " Yes," at once, for he will receive with ease an immediate, but kind, refusal, when, probably, he would cry bitterly at a denial, after his expectations had been raised by suspense.

5*

When a child is to go to bed, we ought not to fret him for the last half hour, by saying every few minutes, "I shall soon send you to bed——Now, my dear, it is time to go——Now, I hope you will go"——but let him be told that, at such a time, he is to go to bed, and when that time arrives, no common excuse should prevent it.

We ought also to be guarded against attaching too much importance to trifles; from this mistake, many an useless combat arises in most nurseries. How often have I observed a a nurse more disturbed, and a child more alarmed and fretted, at a torn or dirty frock, than at a breach of truth, or a want of generosity! Here the lesser good is preferred to the greater, and the primary object of education forgotten.*

* It is much to be regretted that dress is thus often made the subject of dispute and irritation. Personal cleanliness is indeed indispensable; and chil-

By such measures as have been recommended, accompanied by a quick
sympathy with the *peculiar* characters
and peculiar infirmities of children,
much may be done towards forming
among them a *habit* of good temper.
But, such is the irritability both of
the mental and bodily constitution in
childhood, that, with our best efforts,
we must not expect unvarying success.

From some hidden cause, generally
to be traced to their bodily state, many
children, perhaps all occasionally, are
prone to a certain fretfulness, or irritability, which will baffle every attempt
to overcome it, and which, therefore,
is rather to be borne with than op-

dren, whether it teaze them or not, must be thoroughly washed. But their clothes should be so contrived as not to interfere with their freedom and
enjoyment, or to require any great degree of attention. It is desirable to keep them as neat as
the case admits of, but, to do this, a nurse must take
cake care that neither her own temper nor theirs is
sacrificed.

posed—never to be humoured, but to
be received with unmoved serenity
and patience. In such cases, there
appears to be no other method of proceeding. This, indeed, calls for great
patience; but, without great patience,
who can perform the duties required
towards children?

JUSTICE.

"IMPARTIALITY is the life of justice, as justice is of all good government."—It is necessary diligently to enforce upon children principles of strict *justice*, and invariably to act upon them ourselves. We must have no partialities, but give to every one his due; to the elder as much as to the younger; (in this a deficiency may often be observed:) to the unattractive as well as to the more pleasing: each according to his desert, and not according to our own particular feelings. "On every occasion our decisions are to be regulated, not by the *person*, but by the *cause*." We are not to infringe upon the rights of children; remembering that their feelings are a counterpart of our own, and that human nature is the same at every age. It is, therefore, a great, though very common error, to suppose, that, because they are placed under our power, we are not bound by the same laws of justice and honour, in our dealings with them, as with our equals. It is a well-known remark, that " the greatest respect is due to chidren;" and this is especially to be manifesed in a conscientious regard to their just and natural claims. We should hold their little property as more sacred than our own; and insist upon the same principle in their conduct towards each other : not allowing one child to use the playthings of his brother, especially in his absence, without his express consent, teaching them the true import of " thine and mine;" and making it a point of honour to consider the rights of others, as they would their own.

Children ought not to be *obliged* to give and lend :——this is a very frequent mistake. One of them, for example, is eating a cake, and the infant cries for it; the nurse begs for a piece in vain; and, irritated by the unkindness of the one, and the cries of the other, she hastily breaks the cake, and gratifies the desires of the younger, by seizing the property of the elder. The latter feels himself injured; his anger is excited towards his oppressor; and his kind feelings towards his brother impaired:—whilst the former is strengthened in the idea, that, by crying and impatience, he shall obtain the gratification of his wishes. Or, an elder child has a cart; he has played with it till he is tired: the younger begs for the use of it; the elder peremptorily refuses. The nurse persuades; she complains, urges, and remonstrates, till she obtains a reluctant consent;—or, if not, seizes the cart, and gives it to the younger. Here the law of justice is broken;

and the rights of the elder child are violated. It is true, he was unkind and unobliging; but the cart and the cake were his own; and, by taking them from him, without his free and full consent, we shall not teach him generosity, but injustice.

HARMONY, GENEROSITY, &c.

THOROUGHLY to establish the principles of strict justice in the conduct of those who rule, and in that of the children, one toward another, is the grand means of securing the peace and good order of a nursery, and the only sure groundwork of harmony, mutual generosity, and, consequently, of love. The apprehension lest his property should be extorted from him; the fear of having his own rights, in any way, infringed; the suspicion that he may not receive his due, renders a child irritable and contentious; whilst the certainty that he shall himself be treated with entire justice and impartiality, satisfies his mind, composes his spirit, and prepares him to impart, with liberality, what he knows is altogether in his own power. At the same time, the habit of nice attention, on his part,

6

to the rights of others, teaches him the
invaluable lesson of subduing his desires, and of expecting limits to his
individual gratification. Thus the principle of justice, brought into full effect,
cuts off the main sources of dispute and
contention ; prepares the way for a free
and liberal spirit; is the surest preservative against an envious, suspicious temper, and is the first step
towards overcoming that selfishness,
which is the prevailing evil of the
human heart. This evil must be
carefully watched, and perseveringly
counteracted, especially by guarding
against it in our own hearts and behaviour; for, let it be remembered, that
generosity and affection are virtues,
which, from their nature, do not admit of being enforced by authority.
We must not attempt to command
them ; nor should we upbraid children
for the want of them, even towards
ourselves, though we may do much to

promote their growth, by this strict
adherence to justice, by influence, instruction, and a judicious improvement of those natural feelings of kindness, which almost all children occasionally display. There are few who
will not discover emotions of sympathy and pity at the sight of any sorrow or suffering, which they understand to be such; and these are the
occasions for awakening their benevolence and compassion, not only toward their fellow-creatures, but to
every living thing. We should be
particularly careful to lose no such
opportunity of cultivating this tenderness of feeling among themselves. If
one of the little flock be ill, or in pain,
the others will, generally, show an interest and sympathy—a desire to comfort and please him, which should be
carefully cherished. The affections of
elder children are also often called
forth, in a lively manner, toward the

younger. Now, although their attentions to the little one may, at times, be troublesome to the attendant, she ought not hastily to suppress them :—rather let her commend the younger to the care and protection of the elder ; ever bearing in mind the importance of nurturing that *family affection*, so invaluable in the progress of life, and of which the foundation is generally laid within the first ten years of childhood.

Elder children are, on the contrary, sometimes inclined to tease, and domineer over the younger ; though it is commonly those who have themselves been treated with tyranny that are most disposed, in their turn, to become tyrants. This inclination is ever to be repressed : we are to point out the meanness, as well as the barbarity, of employing superior strength, in oppressing, or tormenting, the weak and the helpless ; and uniformly to manifest our abhorrence of cruelty and tyranny, under whatever form they may appear, even when exercised toward the most insignificant insect. Let the first appearances also of a revengeful disposition be especially guarded against, both in our children, and in the conversation and conduct of those who are about them. If a child, in infancy, be encouraged to beat the table, against which he has bruised his head; if he be allowed to strike his brother, from whom he has received a blow; if he hear the language of retaliation, and mutual reproach among his attendants, —can we be surprised, if he display an irascible and vindictive temper, as his will and his passions are strengthened by age?

Although we are not to force upon children even the best instruction, nor urge them to an exertion of self-denial and benevolence, for which their minds

6*

are not ripe; yet we must remember
the importance of raising their views
as they are able to bear it, to the
Christian standard of relative goodness.   We may gradually inculcate
the invaluable precepts, that we should
forgive one another, as we hope ourselves to be forgiven;——that "blessed
are the merciful, for they shall obtain
mercy;" that we are to do to others
as we would have them do to us;
having compassion toward all; being
pitiful and courteous; remembering
" the words of the Lord Jesus," that
" it is more blessed to give than to
receive."

How many of the fairest opportunities will naturally present themselves,
especially to a mother, when the
hearts of her little ones are touched,
not only of inculcating these divine
injunctions, but, which will still more
avail, of tenderly infusing the spirit
they breathe, by sympathy and influ-

ence! Nor is it only the precepts of the New Testament, which may assist us on these occasions, we have also to point out the example of Christ. We have to cultivate the habit of contemplating his character, not only to be loved and admired, as perfect in itself, but as a pattern for us, as the standard at which we are continually to be aiming, as that which is intended to produce the strongest effects upon our lives and affections. It is to be lamented that of this perfect pattern we make so little practical use, that it is so little brought to bear upon the daily conduct of life. No religious instruction is better suited to the minds of children than that derived from the example of Christ, and no part of this example more calculated to touch their hearts, than the compassion, the tenderness, the consideration of the wants

and feelings of others, which he so
perfectly displayed.*

---

* The compassion and tenderness of our Lord
will be strongly illustrated by contrasting them
with the behaviour of the disciples. Excellent as
they were as men, their impatience, and even want
of charity, on many occasions, sufficiently proved
how wide is the difference between human virtue and
divine perfection, between that exalted standard
which is set before us for our imitation, and the
conduct of those who have most nearly approached
to it. It was the language of the disciples, "Send
the multitude away, that they may go into the vil-
lages, and buy themselves victuals." Jesus answered, "Give ye them to eat."—"I have compassion on the multitude: I will not send them
away fasting, lest they faint by the way." (Mat-
thew xiv. and xv.)

The followers of our Lord "charged the blind
man that he should hold his peace." "Jesus stood,
and commanded him to be brought unto him,
saying, What wilt thou that I should do unto thee?
Receive thy sight: thy faith hath saved thee."
(Luke xviii.)

When parents brought their young children to
Jesus, that he should bless them, the disciples re-
buked them. Jesus "was much displeased, and
said unto them, Suffer the little children to come

Children may be easily trained to exercise kindness and liberality towards the poor; they will experience a pleasure in relieving their wants. When old enough, the boys may be induced to save money; the girls to make clothes for the poor families, with whom they are personally acquainted. It is important that the *habit* of giving freely should be early established; for

unto me, and forbid them not. And he took them up in his arms, put his hands upon them, and blessed them." (Mark x.)

When the Samaritans refused to receive their master, the disciples would have commanded fire to come down from heaven to consume them. Jesus answered, "Ye know not what manner of spirit ye are of. For the Son of man is not come to destroy men's lives, but to save them." (Luke ix.)

When his enemies surrounded our Lord with swords and staves, "Simon Peter having a sword drew it, and smote the high priest's servant, and cut off his right ear—then said Jesus unto Peter, Put up thy sword into the sheath." "And he touched his ear and healed him." (John xviii.; Luke xxii.)

the usefulness of many characters is materially abridged through life from the want of this habit. With good and benevolent intentions, they knew not *how* to dispense liberally, or *how* to open their hands freely. Mutual presents, if altogether voluntary, have also a happy tendency in promoting family affection and good will. But, in endeavoring to foster liberality, it must never be forgotten, that *kindness is not to be forced.*

Children, as they advance in age, should be taught to distinguish between that true generosity which involves self-denial, and that which costs them nothing—between a generosity which springs from a desire of applause, and that which is simply the result of benevolence and a sense of duty.

It is desirable that the playthings, books, &c. of each child be marked with his own name: this prevents many disputes, by facilitating that regard to individual property before recommended. When the division of any common treat is left to the children themselves, it is a good regulation that the divider is always to expect the last choice himself; and that the absent are particularly to be remembered—the most liberal shares being reserved for them.

These observations may appear unnecessarily minute; but it is by little things that children acquire habits, and learn to apply general principles:—" To a fond parent, who would not have his son corrected for a perverse trick, but excused it, saying, it was a small matter, Solon wisely replied, ' Aye, but custom is a great one.' "

FEARFULNESS AND FORTITUDE.

IN various characters *fear* assumes *various* forms. Some children, who can brave an external danger, will sink depressed at a reproof or sneer. It is our business to guard against the inroads of fear under every shape; for it is an infirmity, if suffered to gain the ascendency, most enslaving to the mind, and destructive of its strength and capability of enjoyment. At the same time, it is an infirmity so difficult to be overcome, and to which children are so excessively prone, that it may be doubted whether, in any branch of education, more discretion or more skill is required. Indeed I may say that the infirmity once acquired is never totally lost. *Prevent* it then in the beginning of life, for if it once exists, you will never *overcome* it.

We have two objects to keep in

view; the one, to secure our children from all unnecessary and imaginary fears; the other, to inspire them with that strength of mind, which may enable them to meet with patience and courage the real and unavoidable evils of life.

For the first, there is no one who has contemplated the suffering occasioned, through life, by the prevalence of needless fears, imaginary terrors, and diseased nerves, but would most earnestly desire to preserve their children from these evils. To this end, they should be, as far as possible, guarded from every thing likely to excite sudden alarm, or to terrify the imagination. - In very early childhood they ought not to be startled, even at play, by sudden noises or strange appearances. Ghost stories, extraordinary dreams, and all other gloomy and mysterious tales, must on no account be named in their presence : nor must

7

they hear histories of murders, robberies, sudden deaths, mad dogs, or terrible diseases. If any such occurrences are the subjects of general conversation, let them at least be prohibited in the nursery. Nor is it of less importance that we should be cautious ourselves of betraying alarm at storms, a dread of the dark, or a fear and disgust at animals. The stricter vigilance, in these respects, is required, because, by a casual indiscretion on our part; by leaving about an injudicious book; by one alarming story; by once yielding ourselves to an emotion of groundless terror, an impression may be made on the mind of a child that will continue for years, and materially counteract the effect of habitual watchfulness. How cruel, then, *purposely* to excite false terrors in those under our care; as by threatening them with the " black man who comes for naughty children," with "gipsies," "the snake in the well," &c.! Not that children will be long deceived; but when the black man and dreadful monster shall have lost their power, the effect on the imagination, a liability to nervous and undefined terrors, will continue; and thus, for the trifling consideration of sparing ourselves a little present trouble, we entail upon those intrusted to us, suffering, and imbecility of mind, which no subsequent efforts of their own may be able wholly to overcome. We have reason to hope, that the particular expedients here referred to, are, in the present day, excluded from most nurseries; but we may perhaps fall into similar errors, under a more refined form—by exciting, for instance, an apprehension of immediate judgments from heaven, as the consequences of ill conduct. But it is to be remembered that the attempt to touch the conscience, or to enforce obedience by

terrifying the imagination, is, under
every form, to be reprobated, as altogether erroneous and highly injurious.
This mode of proceeding is, commonly
the resort of weakness and inexperi-
ence; for authority, established on
right principles, needs no such supports. Superstitious fears of every
kind are the more to be dreaded, and
earnestly guarded against, because so
peculiarly apt to mingle themselves
with religion, to discolour that which
in its own nature is full of attraction,
and which, if not disguised or distort-
ed by the imagination, would appear, as
it is in truth, a reasonable and joyful
service.

Great care is required that children
do not imbibe terrific and gloomy ideas
of death; nor should they *incautiously*
be taken to funerals, or allowed to see
a corpse. It is desirable to dwell on
the joys of the righteous in the presence of their heavenly Father, freed

from every pain and sorrow, rather than on the state and burial of the body; a subject very likely painfully to affect the imagination. On this point, books are often injudicious. It may be well to mention, as an instance, the Lines on a Snow-drop, in that useful and pleasing little work entitled "Original Poems."* Here the poor little babe, doomed, for ever, to the pit-hole, would leave a gloomy impression on the mind of any child of quick feeling and imagination; it is therefore better to make a point of cutting out such passages from a nursery library.

If children are naturally of a timid, nervous constitution, much may be done toward giving them a healthful

* The author has often regretted that, in making this observation, she did not at the same time express her sense of obligation to the authors of " Original Poems, Nursery Rhymes and Hymns," having, for many years, experienced the value of these little books as sources of instruction and amusement in the nursery.

7*

tone of mind ;—but it must be effected
by more than common skill, and by
measures the most gentle and unper-
ceived. Direct opposition, upbraiding
a child for his cowardice, accusing him
of fearing the dark; of believing in
ghosts, &c., will but establish, or perhaps create, the very evils we desire to
counteract. If a child dread the dark,
he must on no account be forced into
it, or left in bed against his will without
a candle. We had better appear neither to see his weakness, nor consider
it of importance, and for a time silently
yield to it, rather than notice or oppose
it : at the same time, losing no opportunity of infusing a counteracting principle. He may very soon be tempted
to join his bolder companions in a dark
room at a game of play, or to hunt for
sugar-plums, especially if his mother or
nurse will join the sport, till he become
accustomed to it.——Well chosen stories,
without any apparent reference to him-

self, may be related to him, displaying the good effects of courage, as opposed to the folly and ill consequence of cowardice. As he advances in age and strength of mind, he will be able to profit by some reasoning on the subject. We may animate him to overcome his fears by an exertion of his own, encouraging him by rewards and approbation; but let the efforts which he makes be wholly voluntary, and not by constraint.

It is not uncommon, with the idea of removing the groundless fears of children, to give them histories of strange, terrific, or perhaps ghost-like appearances, to be in the sequel cleared up and explained away. But experience will convince us that this is a very mistaken system; for, in childhood, the imagination is quick and retentive, but the reasoning powers are slow and weak. The alarming image and nervous impression may continue, whilst the subsequent explanation and practical inference will most likely be forgotten.

There are few more fruitful sources of fearfulness than mystery; it is therefore a mistake to assume an air of concealment towards children—to speak in their presence by hints, or in a suppressed voice, on subjects unsuited to them. We are apt also to forget how many things are to them fearful and mysterious, which experience has rendered to us familiar and simple. In the course of conversation, and amidst the common occurrences of life, many things will strike the mind and even the senses of a child as strange and alarming, merely because he understands them but by halves; and this not unfrequently arises from the thoughtless manner in which we are apt to speak before children of distressing circumstances, as of terrible diseases and other calamities. Such im-

pressions, when perceived, ought neither to be ridiculed, nor carelessly overlooked.   We should endeavour to
ascertain from what they proceed, and
to state the subject in question in so
simple and familiar a manner as may
strip it of its alarming character.   To
succeed in this, it will be necessary to
cultivate that quick penetration which
readily understands the looks and manners of children, a language which
often conveys more than their words. I
had a few weeks since, an example of
this with a little boy of my own, about
five years old.   He was walking with
me in the dusk of the evening; as we
passed one corner of the garden, I
found my hand squeezed more tightly,
and an inclination to cling to my side,
but nothing was said; in returning to
the same spot, this was again and
again repeated.   I was certain it must
arise from an emotion of fear, though I
could perceive nothing likely to pro-

duce it. I would not however pass it over, and at length induced my little companion to confess, " Mamma! I think I see under that bush an animal with very great ears!" I immediately approached the object, gently persuaded him to follow me, when we found, to our amusement, a large tin watering pot, and "the very great ears" converted into the spout and handle. Had the squeeze of the hand been unheeded, a fearful association with the dark, and with that spot in the garden, would, there is little doubt, long have continued.

In endeavoring to guard those under our care from *fearfulness*, we are not to forget the importance of inspiring them with *prudence*.

Fearfulness does but embitter life with the useless dread of evils which cannot or may not happen—prudence promotes our safety, by teaching us to use all reasonable precautions against

positive evils. While, therefore, we
do our utmost to secure our children
from useless fears, we should strongly
but coolly warn them against real
dangers, as those from fire, water, &c.
Although prudence and fearfulness are
sometimes confounded, it is remarkable
how often they act in direct opposition
to each other, the coward being hurried
by his groundless or imaginary terrors
into actual dangers.

"Fortitude is not only essential as a Christian
virtue in itself, but as a guard to every other
virtue." LOCKE.

Although, by securing our children
from useless fears and alarming impressions, we gain the first step toward the cultivation of courage and
fortitude, yet this alone is not sufficient. If we would insure the attainment of these excellent endowments,
it will be necessary to infuse into our
system of education a certain portion

of resolution and hardihood.   We must bear in mind, that we have to train up those intrusted to us, not for a life of rewards, ease, and pleasure; but for a world in which they will meet with pain, sickness, danger and sorrow: that we are bringing them up, not only to be useful in the various engagements of this life; but chiefly to carry on that great work, the salvation of their souls, in which fortitude and self-denial are essential!

Although we cannot be too careful to promote the happiness of children, an object surely too often neglected in education, yet do we not defeat our purpose, in proportion as we unfit them for the life upon which they are entering, by too tender and enervating a system? By so doing, we increase their sensibility to pain, whilst we add nothing to their sources of true enjoyment. It is the path of wisdom to steer between opposite evils, avoiding on the one hand every appearance of unkindness, or a want of feeling and sympathy—on the other, a fostering to excess an over-indulgence—a morbid anxiety and sensibility. "We should distinguish between the wants of nature and caprice," bringing up our children as little dependent as possible upon bodily indulgence and luxuries; accustoming them to the plainest food, to hard beds, airy rooms, and, as far as their constitution will allow of it, to hardy habits. That tendency to self-indulgence, daintiness and waste, so often to be observed in those who are living in the midst of affluence, is to be carefully repressed in early life. Something, perhaps, may be done towards this important end by positive restraints; but how much more effectually shall we accomplish our purpose, if we can form such habits and establish such principles as will lead chil-

8

dren to deny themselves! Nor will it be difficult to represent to them, that a lavish and intemperate use of the gifts of our heavenly Father is a species of ingratitude to him, and of injustice to those of our fellow-creatures who need the blessings so abundantly bestowed upon us.

We should endeavour to furnish children with a shield against the lesser pains—the daily portion of vexation and disappointment, from which even the happiest childhood is not exempt, and thus to prepare them for the more serious trials of advanced life. We must beware of giving heed to the language of murmuring or discontent, "cheering but not bemoaning them" under their little misfortunes, and especially discouraging the habit of crying and fretting on every slight accident and passing pain; for such a habit induces effeminacy of character, and the self-government required to suppress complaints and tears, is strengthening to the mind, and calculated to lead on, by lesser victories, to nobler efforts hereafter.

When children are sick, or in pain, whilst doing our utmost to relieve, to solace, and to divert them, it is yet necessary, *for their sakes*, hard as it may be to ourselves, to mingle resolution with our tenderness : for if, by an excess of indulgence, by too great a display of sympathy, we weaken the mind or spoil the temper, in that proportion we add to their sufferings ; and I believe it will generally be found, as I was convinced myself by the painful experience of many months, that some discipline, *combined with the tenderest attentions*, is as necessary for the comfort of children in sickness as in health. It is also of importance, early to encourage them to submit with resolution to the necessary infliction of painful remedies, and to think lightly of them, as tooth-drawing, taking medicine, and using other means which often form a considerable part of the trial of sickness.

In bringing up children at home, care is required that they should not imbibe a sense of self importance and personal superiority. In domestic families, secluded from general society, this is by no means an unfrequent evil. The little ones, being in fact the primary object to their parents, imperceptibly catch the feeling, and are discomposed when put out of their own way, or thrown into the back ground; whereas an important branch of the hardihood of mind, so much to be desired in children, is that self-subjection which induces a readiness "to take the lowest place," and to yield their own inclinations for the accommodation of their superiors. The hourly exercise of self-denial, and the necessity of considering the interests of others which arise from living in a community, greatly promote this invaluable temper; and if all education require " sound wisdom and discretion," a double portion is needed with a single child.

We shall succeed in the early cultivation of fortitude and patience, chiefly by influence, and the careful formation of habits. There are certain principles, however, relating to the subjects before us, not to be prematurely brought forward, but ever to be kept in view; thoroughly to be established in our own minds, and strongly impressed upon those of our children, as their powers strengthen and opportunities offer. These are the principles of overcoming self, of struggling against natural infirmities, of enduring present pain for the sake of future good, and still more, of humble submission to the will of God, receiving, as from the hand of a gracious father,

8*

not only our many comforts and blessings, but the portion of sorrow and disappointment which he sees meet to dispense to us for our good. When inculcating principles, we shall find it a great assistance with children, to enforce them by examples, and to engage the feelings and imagination by interesting narratives, which may illustrate our instructions and elevate the mind. Such, on the subject before us, are the stories in Evenings at Home, on "True Heroism," and "Perseverance against Fortune,"—many parts of Sandford and Merton, and of "True Stories for Children"—selections from the lives of eminent men, as of Howard, &c. From profane history, as the accounts of Regulus, of the citizens of Calais, &c. From the characters of Scripture; as Abraham's and Eli's submission, Stephen's martyrdom; and above all, from the life and death of Him who set us a perfect "example that we should follow his steps," whose history is indeed too sacred to be rendered common, but must be imparted to children as they are able to relish and to enter into it.

I would venture to remind those engaged in the work of education, of the necessity of practising themselves that fortitude and patience, which they are desirous of cultivating in their young charges. A mother especially, and in her feelings an affectionate nurse will closely participate, is vulnerable at so many points; the objects of her tenderest affection are exposed to so many diseases, so many hazards, that she may become the prey to endless fears, equally painful to herself and injurious to her children, without the habitual exercise of self-government and principle—a principle founded on the conviction that it is not in ourselves to preserve life and health;

that, with all our care and vigilance, it
is comparatively little we can do, and
that after taking every reasonable pre-
caution, our only lasting resource is
to commit ourselves, and those nearest
to us, to Him "in whom we live and
move, and have our being," who hath
numbered the very hairs of our head,
and who suffereth not even a spar-
row to fall to the ground without him.
It is not sufficient barely to acknowledge these divine truths; they must
be "inwardly digested," and formed
into practical principles, to enable a
tender parent to prepare her children
for "the warfare of life," and to meet
with composure and submission the
vicissitudes and anxieties necessarily
attendant on bringing up a family.
Nor is the utter fruitlessness of excessive care to be forgotten : such care,
by enervating the mind and weakening
the body, altogether defeats its own
end, making way for the very evils it

would guard against; and what is
more pitiable than the state of that
child, who, having imbibed his mother's sensations, lives a prey to the
continual dread of the common casual-
ties of life!

It may be well here to add a particular caution to nurses, who are too
often inclined, in times of sickness and
solicitude, to give way to their own
feelings, and thus to unfit themselves
for rendering the help and support so
much needed by the mother, as well as
by their little patients. A tearful or
melancholy countenance has in itself a
depressing effect, and a steady cheerful temper of mind is almost as important a requisite in a nurse as tenderness
and affection. Some minds are naturally endowed with such a portion of
fortitude, as enables them to meet with
comparative ease the roughness and
trials of life; but with most of us so
invaluable an attainment is to be ac-

quired only by diligent cultivation; by little and little, by many efforts and daily practice, by previous preparation and habit of mind, rather than by a sudden effort at the moment of trial. It is a remark of no small moment, that " health should be the preparation for sickness, and prosperity for adversity." We should labour, therefore, to acquire an habitual composure, self-possession, and presence of mind, and as far as possible to impart the same to our children ; to be always quiet, quick in applying the necessary remedies, not yielding to sudden alarms and agitations; never indulging in the injurious habit of screaming, or uttering exclamations, on the various accidents of a nursery; nor urging as a plea for such failures, *a weakness of nerves.* This, in the present day, is often brought forward as a cover for infirmities which are rather to be condemned, and resolutely overcome, than palliated or indulged.

It is desirable for parents, and those intrusted with the care of children, to instruct themselves in the best method of proceeding, under the sudden disease and dangers to which children are the most liable, as convulsions, choking, wounds, profuse bleeding, accidents from fire, water,* &c.

* See Dr. Aikin's chapter on Presence of Mind in his "Evenings at Home."

INDEPENDENCE.

Connected with that strength of character, the cultivation of which has been recommended, is independence. It will be of great advantage to children if they are early induced to put forth their powers; to resort first to the resources within themselves; and, as far as possible, to obtain their objects by their own exertions. Such an exercise strengthens the faculties, and gradually prepares a child for acting alone; whilst the habit of having every thing done for him, of depending upon others for all his enjoyments, enervates the mind, and has a tendency to weaken the active powers. The " I can't," with which children are apt to reply to the commands given them, is rarely to be admitted. " I can't," is too often brought forward merely as an excuse for indolence, or an apology for disobedience. Our pupils must learn that success depends upon resolute exertion; and, that under certain limitations it is a truth, that man *can* do what he *chooses* to do. This conviction adopted as a practical principle will be powerful in its effects; and will materially contribute to improve the capacities, and augment the usefulness of any character.* Children will act with prudence, will employ and take care of themselves, very much in proportion as we lead them to do so; we must manifest our confidence in them, if we would render them worthy of it.

* " John Hunter, the celebrated surgeon, being asked by what methods he had contrived to succeed in all his various undertakings, answered, ' My rule is deliberately to consider, before I commence, whether the thing be practicable. If it be not practicable, I do not attempt it; if it be practicable, I can accomplish it, if I give sufficient pains to it—and having begun, I never stop till the thing is done. To this rule I owe all my success.' "

Where can we find a being more helpless, more unable to contrive for himself, to guard against danger, or to
escape from it when it comes upon
him, than a child who has been brought
up by his mother's or his nurse's side ;
looking to her for every enjoyment, and
feeling his safety to be wholly dependent on her care? On the other hand,
it may excite surprise to observe how
much good sense and self possession
children will display when early accustomed to depend upon themselves.
This object, like every other connected
with education, is not to be attained by
great efforts, but gradually, and by
gentle measures. We are not to impose upon children that which is beyond their strength and skill ; but we
may lead them to take pleasure in accomplishing their objects without assistance, to feel it a point of honour to
pursue them, notwithstanding some
difficulties ; to extricate themselves,

to submit to trouble, and to surmount
obstacles.

As it is by the "neglect of beginnings" that bad habits are contracted,
we should not overlook even those
minor occurrences of life, which early
afford opportunities for inculcating a
spirit of independence. For example
a little child runs to the door, impa-
tiently turns and twists the handle, but
cannot open it; the nurse springs up
and does it for him. But it would have
been better had she kindly encouraged
him to exert his own skill, and with the
aid of her instructions to effect his purpose. He may by degrees take care
of, and put away his own playthings,
dress himself, &c.; but in urging him to
these little efforts, care will be required that they do not carry it so far as to
make them too serious a business, or
to try his temper. As he advances in
age, let him in his walks climb the gate
and hedge along; attend to his own

garden; saddle his own pony; and, as far as he is able, find amusements for himself in his play hours. When it can be done with safety, he may occasionally be intrusted with the care of a younger brother or sister. This has a tendency to endear children to each other; the elder feels the younger to be under his particular protection, whilst the younger looks up to his brother for help and defence. By cultivating these sentiments, we may check the oppression, teasing, and conquently disputes, so common between the elder and younger children of a family.

It is not unfrequently the case that mothers and nurses are pleased by the unqualified dependence of those under their care, and, for self gratification, encourage it at the expense of their children. They strive to retain their influence, and to secure a selfish affec-

tion, by rendering their darlings helpless, and by fostering their babyish
habits.   But it is to be remembered,
that general independence and vigour
of character are perfectly compatible
with the *dependence of affections*. This,
indeed, is an object of first-rate importance, and must necessarily spring
out of that tenderest connection—the
connection between a mother and her
children; it must be the result of those
innumerable kindnesses, of that flow of
love and sympathy, which an affectionate and judicious mother cannot but
uniformly display toward her children.
Such a mother needs not the aid of a
morbid dependence to retain her influence; she has no occasion to nurture
the infirmities of her children, that she
may strengthen their affection.   It is
to be desired that children should possess the greatest tenderness toward a
mother, an enjoyment and delight in
her society, a reverence for her opi-

9*

nions, and submission to her authority, combined with power to act alone, and to pursue their independent objects with vigour and pleasure; for it is necessary to all, but more especially to boys, that they should mingle strength with affection; that they should be manly as well as tender, and be trained to help, as well as to be helped.

INDUSTRY, PERSEVERANCE, AND ATTENTION.

As idleness is the inlet to most other evils, so it is by industry that the powers of the mind are turned to good account. That so little is effected by most people, may be attributed much more to the waste and misapplication than to the want of natural powers ; and it will generally be found that usefulness of character depends more upon diligence than any thing else, if we except religious principle. It is therefore highly important to train up children to habits of industry, application, and perseverance. They should early be made sensible of the infinite value of time ; they should be made to understand that no economy is so essential as the economy of time ; and

that, as by squandering pence we are
very soon deprived of pounds, so by
wasting minutes we shall lose not only
hours, but days and months. They
ought not, therefore, to be allowed to
remain idle, " because it is not worth
while" to undertake any employment ;
for this is an excuse often brought
forward during those intervals of time
which occur in the course of almost
every day. We are mistaken, if we
suppose that industry is to be confined
to lesson hours : children may be as
idle when at play as over their books :
we must therefore take care that the
time devoted to relaxation be properly and happily employed. The first
dawnings of a listless, dissatisfied dis-
-position, are to be checked : such a
propensity will lead a child to loll in
his chair, to stretch on the ground,
rather than trouble himself to join in
the games of his more active companions : it will lead him to seek for

amusement, first in one thing, then in another; but to rest content with none. To counteract this tendency, it is necessary to supply children with pleasurable objects—varied, but not too numerous—and to encourage a vigorous and persevering pursuit of them. It is desirable, if in the country, that they should have gardens of their own, tools, a pony, &c.; and we shall find it an important advantage, if we are able to inspire them with a taste for reading *as an amusement.* This will be promoted by the habit of buying and collecting books for themselves; each child enjoying the privilege of a little library of his own.

One of the duties of a nurse is to employ her charges well in the absence of their parents. If, for example, she provide herself with paper, pencils, paints, little pictures, &c. to cut out and paste, as employment for wet days and winter evenings, many hours may be spent harmoniously and happy, which in an ill-regulated nursery would pass in idleness, and, consequently quarreling and mischief. For children who are brought up in domestic and natural habits, it will not be difficult to find an abundant variety of wholesome and simple pleasures; and we should carefully avoid exciting a desire for artificial amusements, which, if they produce no other ill consequence, are, like all unnecessary stimulants, enervating in their effects, vitiating to the taste, and likely to abate the relish for more common and more valuable enjoyments. Among such objectionable amusements are to be ranked those of the theatre, cards, and every species of infantine gaming.*

* By "infantine gaming" it is intended to include only those games in which children play for money, or which, at least, may lead to their doing so at some future period.

We must endeavor to inspire children with the spirit inculcated in the
following precept—"Whatsoever thy
hand findeth to do, do it with thy
might," (*Eccles.* ix. 10,) to bring them
gradually "to be a whole man to every
thing." This is an acquirement fraught
with the most important advantages,
though of very difficult attainment. So
volatile is the mind during childhood,
so averse to restraint, that it is only
by very slow degrees the habits here
recommended can be formed. We
must not expect complete success
with any children, and with some the
difficulty will appear nearly insur-
mountable. Energy of mind, like
power in mechanism, if once attained,
may be directed and applied to a variety of objects; but the want of this
energy—an indifference, a spiritless-
ness of character—is a defect most
difficult to be overcome. Our ordinary resources are apt to fail with

minds of this cast; for with them
the hope of obtaining a desired object,
the wish for rewards, the love of reputation, and even a sense of duty, will
readily yield to every difficulty, and
rarely triumph over that aversion to
labour, which, if suffered to prevail,
has a tendency to undermine whatever is excellent or valuable. In the
treatment of children of this character, a double portion of patience and
perseverance is required; and, with
all our efforts, we may appear to effect very little; but that little will
probably lead to more. We must observe their tastes; and, if possible,
excite activity, by presenting them
with objects which particularly accord
with their inclination. We may sometimes, with those of good dispositions,
accomplish our purpose, by engaging
their affections, and working upon
love more than upon fear. It will
also be especially necessary to guard

against that deceit which is too often the consequence of indolence; for a child habitually indolent, will make it his object to get through every employment, particularly his lessons, with as little trouble to himself as possible; and the consciousness of his deficiencies—the consciousness of having failed in duty, will almost inevitably induce him to take refuge in falsehood or mean excuses. We should therefore, as far as possible, avoid trusting such children to learn their lessons alone; for this will be exposing them to temptation. Let it be an object to give them employments which they cannot evade—from which there are no means of escaping: something to be *done*, and not merely to be *learnt*. For instance, it will be better to set them so many lines to write, rather than to learn by heart. If tasks must be set, they should be made as short, as defined, as mechanical as pos-

sible, and learnt in the presence of the
teacher.   To all children, perhaps, the
rudiments of learning may be made
easier, by rendering them as mechanical as the subject admits of.   It may
be better not to tell a little child, that
he shall spell his lessons till he does
it without a mistake ; but to desire
him to spell it so many times over,
aloud and distinctly, as the business
of the day.——Children will also learn
more readily, when their lessons are
regulated by established rules.   If a
child be uncertain how much he is to
read, he will probably murmur when
the portion is shown to him.   Rather
let it be fixed, that, to read so much
——to spell so many words so many
times, &c., is to be the regular business of every day.   He will then come
with a prepared mind, which is as important to the success and good temper of children as of ourselves.   On
this account a daily perseverance in

teaching, and regular hours, are necessary. The habit of omitting lessons on every slight excuse, has an injurious effect; and a child will come very unwillingly to be taught, who, from his past experience, daily hopes that he may put off the task, or escape it altogether.

It ought to be our object, that our pupils should advance *surely*, rather than *rapidly*. The most important advantage of lessons—of regular, daily lessons in childhood, is this:—That they afford us an excellent opportunity of enforcing habits of self-subjection, diligence and attention, and an opportunity of cultivating a taste for intellectual pursuits. In the first ten years of life, it is not the quantity of knowledge acquired, but the habit of learning well, that is of consequence. With very young children, however, even this principle is to be acted upon with moderation. It is a rule that such a portion should be read, spelt, &c.; and our object is to have this portion done *well :* but we must be prepared for constant fluctuations in our little pupils. The fixed portion of business must, indeed, be done; and if we perceive a spirit of self-will and disobedience, this must be corrected. But that our pupils will be at one time more industrious; at another, less so; at one time vigorous; at another, listless; at one time, quick; at another, apparently slow and dull—must be expected : it is the nature, the constitution of children. These changes are to be borne with unruffled patience and quietness, and expressions of displeasure carefully avoided; for it is hurtful, and utterly useless, to upbraid children with dulness and inattention. Let us get through the lesson—get through it as well as we can; and then, if the child display no positive naughtiness, leave it. The fixed portion of business being completed, the child is to be dismissed; and there is little doubt we shall accomplish more at some future period.

But the self-love of parents and teachers is very apt to insinuate itself into this employment. We do not like that other children should read and write better than ours; we are mortified at not gaining the immediate fruit of our labour—that the directions given to-day are not practised to-day. Our pupil seldom keeps pace with our impatience; this irritates the temper, and brings down complaints and punishments upon the poor child, for defects which often arise more from a want of power, than a want of will. Thus, so painful an association with his books is excited, as may prove of serious disadvantage to him in after life. This mistake is generally to be observed in young mothers, and those unaccustom-

10*

ed to the infirmities of childhood. It should be remembered, that the actual result of each individual lesson is of little importance, if no bad habits are formed, or wrong tempers excited. It is by a long succession of lessons that progress will be perceived; by "line upon line, and precept upon precept." Not that we are to expect that children can be properly taught without discipline, or that the whole of learning can be rendered merely an amusement. Some objects absolutely require labour and self-subjection; but at the same time there is no doubt that a judicious teacher, with many children, may excite a great deal of spirit in learning, and may impart instruction on a variety of subjects so as to interest and delight rather than fatigue. If once we are able to enlist in the cause the inclination of a child, the chief difficulty is removed: there will be little doubt of his success, and we render him a lasting service. How careful, then, should we be to make learning as agreeable as possible, to beware of exciting disgust towards study, and to nurture a literary taste, not only as good in itself, but as an important preservative from evil, especially to boys, in future life!

It is to be regretted, that the common mode of teaching has more to do with the memory than the understanding. With many children whose innumerable "tasks are painfully learnt and darkly understood," the memory is exercised, not to say burthened, whilst the real cultivation of the mind, the improvement of the reasoning powers, and the formation of good intellectual habits, are overlooked.* Is it not to

* See Locke on the Conduct of the Understanding, and Watts on the Mind; books from which many excellent hints may be derived on the subject of education. Of the latter, Dr. Johnson remarks, "Few books have been perused by me with greater pleasure than Watts's Improvement

this cause that often may be attributed the imperfect and superficial knowledge, the want of literary taste, in those who have been taught merely by the common school routine—and is it not desirable that such deficiencies be remedied as far as possible, during the intervals of time passed at home, by directing the attention to English reading—to the study of natural history, and other interesting pursuits? As it is sensible objects which the soonest attract attention in early life, the works of nature may easily be rendered the medium of continual instruction and amusement to children. On this account, natural history, in its various branches, is particularly useful, as both pleasure and improvement may be derived from the habit of observing and

of the Mind. Whoever has the care of instructing others, may be charged with deficiency in his duty, if this book is not recommended."

examining the various objects with which we are surrounded.*

A high standard is desirable in intellectual pursuits, as well as in those of still greater value. Nothing can be less ornamental than accomplishments performed in a poor style, and with bad taste, or than that superficial and perfect knowledge which

"——is proud that it has learnt so much."

But whilst we endeavour to inspire our children with a desire to do well whatever they undertake, whilst we endeavour to turn to the best account both their time and talents, we must beware of raising our expectations too high ; for, if an ambitious spirit insinuate itself into the business of education, it will be a source of mortification

* The advantages of such a habit are displayed in that highly interesting work, White's Natural History of Selborne ; and in the story of Evenings at Home, entitled " Eyes and no Eyes."

to the parent, and of irritation to the children It is but too probable that in this case the latter will be over-urged by the former: and, thus, those very objects frustrated which have been pursued with too much eagerness.

In cultivating habits of industry, application, and perseverance, we are to remember that there is a medium to be observed in this, as in every other branch of education. These qualities are of so much value, that they demand a full share of our attention: but we are not so to pursue them, as to infringe upon the necessary liberty and the truest enjoyment of children. It ought again to be repeated, that *all unnecessary restraint is only so much unnecessary evil.* We must also treat with much tenderness, that lassitude and apparent indolence, which even slight indisposition will occasion in children. In the short time devoted to lessons, we may gradually employ a stricter discipline; but in play hours, although it is a positive duty strongly to oppose listlessness and indolence; yet, with healthy and well-trained children, we shall find little else necessary than to direct their activities, to encourage their projects, and to add to their pleasures.

VANITY AND AFFECTATION.

THERE are few defects which appear
earlier than vanity. Children delight
in being noticed and admired; and it
is therefore of importance, that amidst
all our affectionate attentions to them,
all our efforts for their good and happiness, we guard against nurturing
their self-love, self-importance, and
fondness for admiration. Children
ought to be the objects of our assiduous attention—we should be willing to give up our time, not only for
the more serious business of education, but to please, to amuse, and to
make them happy. This, however,
may be done without throwing back
their attention on themselves. We may
show them every kindness without flat-
tering their vanity; but here many
people are apt to mistake: their no-

tice is bestowed in so injudicious a manner. If, for instance, upon the entrance of children into a room, a general whisper of approbation go round the circle ; if remarks are made on their persons, their carriage, and their manner ; if their sayings are eagerly listened to and *repeated in their presence*, the ill effect is inevitable.

Praise and encouragement, judiciously and sparingly administered, will have effects very different from those produced by the kind of notice here objected to. The one injures whilst it pleases, leading the subjects of it to think of themselves, and exciting a self-complacency, which is very soon followed by display ; the other is a just reward of merit, and a stimulus to what is good. In bestowing praise, however, even when most deserved, we should bear in mind the great importance of leading our chil-

11

dren to a habit of examining their *motives*, of doing right from a sense of duty, rather than from the love of applause, or the desire of excelling others. Whilst we stimulate to exertion, care must at the same time be taken to uphold the beauty of humility as the chief ornament of childhood; but unless this, in some measure, exist in our own hearts, unless we ourselves are influenced by that meek and quiet spirit which is in the sight of God of great price, there is little hope that we shall succeed in our endeavours to foster it in others.

An excess of personal vanity is rarely to be overcome by direct opposition, or positive restraint. We shall be more likely to succeed in counteracting such a disposition, by allowing to external appearance its due value, its due share of attention—by inculcating *general moderation* in every selfish gratification, and still more, by improving the tone of mind, and raising it to higher tastes and better objects. Dress should be treated as a matter of very secondary importance; new and smart clothes ought not to be offered as a reward for good conduct; and whether they are to be of one shape, or another, this colour or that, is never to be brought forward as an affair of consequence. Too much restraint on this subject generally defeats its own end, and renders dress, just what we should wish it not to be, an object of unnecessary thought and attention. The desire to please, so strongly implanted in the heart, must be allowed to have some play, and, when kept within due bounds, is not to be despised or treated as a fault; whilst we strictly avoid all that is incorrect or extravagant, we should not, unnecessarily, expose our children to the pain and awkwardness of feeling themselves singular in manner and appearance.

Closely connected with vanity is affectation, to which children are also exceedingly prone. Nothing can be more delightful than the innocent prattle and merriment of a child, when it flows simply from the gayety of his heart—we should encourage it, and be merry with him; but if we have the weakness, may we not say the unkindness, to let him see that he is an object of attention and admiration, to put him upon showing off his pretty ways, for the amusement of our friends, or allow it to be done for the laugh of the kitchen; we gain our object indeed, he is sprightly and talkative, but no longer because he is gay at heart, but because he longs to be noticed and admired—and this is affectation. Those who are accustomed to children will be able quickly to discern affectation, not only in their words and actions, but even in their looks, and should *always* disappoint it—*always* receive it with coldness and disapprobation.

We shall succeed very imperfectly in securing our children from vanity and affectation, unless we first set a guard upon our own conduct—unless we ourselves are acting from better motives than the love of admiration, or the desire of excelling others; unless our own manners are simple and natural. If it be the main object of those who are engaged in education, that themselves or their children should please and excel, a similar spirit will most likely show itself in the objects of their care. If we allow ourselves to speak in affected tones of voice; fondling our children to excess, and using extravagant expressions of affection and admiration, a defect so frequent amongst nurses, something answering to it will certainly appear in

11*

them; for we shall find that they are wonderfully alive to sympathy and imitation; quick in discerning what passes before them, especially if it regard themselves, and, when we least suppose it, strongly affected by the conduct and feeling of those around them.

DELICACY.

On this subject there is little to be said; for it is only those who have refined and delicate feelings, who shrink from all that is coarse or impure, and who desire for themselves to be " wise unto that which is good, and simple concerning evil," who can fully appreciate so invaluable a spirit in their children, or who would know how to guard it in them as the choicest plant, though of the tenderest growth. If children are tempted to commit other faults, if they are misled into other errors, there is great hope that the voice of conscience will be heard, and bring them back to the path of duty : but if the purity of the mind be sullied or lost, this cannot be regained ; the outward conduct may be correct ; but a beauty, a charm—a security to all that is good, is gone,

The necessity of giving children good principles is generally acknowledged, but the importance of inspiring them with good *tastes* is much oftener overlooked. A correct *moral taste* will not only prove an invaluable aid to religious principle, but will be a safeguard against the inroads of corruption, even when religion has but too little influence on the heart. Purity of character is so little in unison with the spirit of the world, that, unless carefully cherished and watched over, we cannot hope to retain it; and it is on this account more than on any other, that companions for children should be selected with the greatest care; that unguarded intercourse with others is to be dreaded; low company prohibited; and that peculiar discernment and discretion are necessary in the choice of those to whose care they are intrusted.

During the first ten years of life, it is generally the case both with boys and girls, that the character is chiefly formed by female influence; and how well calculated *ought* that influence to prove, to foster the purity and innocence of childhood! It is only to be lamented that women, both in the higher and lower walks of life, should endanger that refined delicacy, so essential to their character, by ever allowing themselves to treat what is impure as a subject of curiosity or amusement; by admitting conversation which is not perfectly delicate; by reading books of an improper tendency, or by devouring promiscuously the contents of our public papers.*

Even little children are sometimes inclined, in their measure, to indelicate conversation, and will indulge in it, for the amusement of each other, and to

* Perhaps no amusement can be less suitable than this for elder children, or young people, especially girls, and it is surprising that newspapers are so often intrusted to them.

excite a laugh : but in nothing has a license of tongue a more corrupting effect; and any tendency to indelicacy in words or actions, is one of the few things in children which ought to be treated with severity. An incorrect word, or an improper trick, in infancy, may at the time be amusing, as appearing to spring from childish playfulness and humour : but here an object of no small importance is at stake ; we are to manifest our disapprobation both towards the offender and those who are amused at his fault, and we must take care that our looks correspond with our conduct; for a secret smile will more than counteract the effect of the severest reproof.

A great deal on the subject before us will depend on the nice principles, the correct propriety, and the constant watchfulness of a nurse : for it is by a strict and minute attention to little things, that modest and refined habits are formed, and a disgust induced at all that is improper and vulgar. A nurse cannot be too much guarded in what she does or says in the presence of her children, nor must she fancy that they are always infants or less alive than herself, to what passes before them. At the same time, the precautions taken should be perceived as little as possible; for she will defeat her end, if she excite curiosity by giving the idea that there is something to be concealed.

Diligence and regular employment are great safeguards to purity, for it is the indolent and vacant mind that is the most susceptible of improper impressions.

When children ask embarrassing questions, we are not to deceive them, or resort to a falsehood that we may keep them in ignorance. If we receive such questions with an unmoved countenance, and seeming indifference;

without the least air of mystery or concealment, and with no apparent awkwardness or confusion; we may answer them with truth, though perhaps only in part, without exciting further curiosity, or improperly opening their minds, and we may easily prevent their pursuing the subject, by diverting their thoughts to other objects. It is also to be remembered, that there are some things which it is safer for children to learn from their parents, than from those who are less judicious and less guarded; for in many cases, it is not so much the matter of fact, as an improper spirit in conveying it, which is injurious to the mind.

MANNERS AND ORDER.

LOCKE considers that manner is the object of next importance to religion and virtue, to be preferred to learning; and it is evident that there is no passport so good in the world—nothing that adds so great a lustre to virtue, or that so well brings into daily use more solid acquirements. "Good manners are the blossom of good sense," and, may it not be added, of good feeling too; for, if the law of kindness be written in the heart, it will lead to that disinterestedness in little as well as in great things—that desire to oblige, and attention to the gratification of others, which is the foundation of good manners. If, therefore, we are successful in inspiring children with such a disposition, we secure the most important means of rendering them pleasing.

12

We should endeavour early to infuse the spirit of that precept—"Honour all men;" to teach them that kindness and civility are due to all; that a haughty, peremptory, or contemptuous manner is not only ill-bred, but unchristian; and that this is especially to be guarded against in their behaviour to servants. Nor will young people, generally, be tempted to treat with unkindness those whose services claim a return of affection and gratitude, unless they are led to it by the example of others.

It will also be necessary to guard children against vulgar habits, against roughness of manner, as well as coarseness of mind; as loud talking and laughing, the use of violent exclamations and expressions, "shocking! terrible! monstrous!" &c.; nor should they be allowed to continue their infantine language too long: the imperfect words and broken sentences of an infant will be unpleasant, and appear like affectation, when used by elder children; but this habit is often encouraged by the affected and babyish tones of voice, in which their attendants frequently address them. It is essential to good breeding that children be taught to express themselves well, and to speak distinctly and grammatically.

As satire and ridicule are instruments ill calculated to be employed in education, so any tendency to these dispositions in children themselves is to be repressed; mimickry also, though highly amusing, ought to be discouraged, as being likely to induce an unpleasing and improper turn of mind.

Good conduct at meals is, with children a fair criterion of good manners, and meals may be made use of as favourable opportunites for inculcating propriety of behaviour. Children should be taught to sit down and rise

up from table, at the same time; to
wait whilst others are served, without
betraying eagerness or impatience; to
avoid noise and conversation; and, if
they are no longer confined to the nursery, to be able to see delicacies without expecting or asking to partake of
them.   To know when to be silent, is
more important to good manners than
is generally supposed. Speaking, when
it interrupts reading or conversation,
the and habit of contradicting others,
should be checked, as also that ill-timed
garrulity, so unpleasing in some children, and which generally springs from
an undesirable self-confidence and forwardness of character.

Nor is the *person* to be neglected in
early life; for it will spare children
many awkward feelings as they grow
up, if they are taught to walk and to
carry themselves well; to enter and
leave a room, and to address others,

with ease and propriety. With many, the acquirement of this external polish will prove a very slow work, and a subject of considerable difficulty; but if we see an amiable and obedient disposition, there is every reason to hope that roughness of manner will be smoothed down by time and the example of others. Parents ought not, therefore, to allow themselves, from their own irritability and impatience, to render *manner*, as is the case in so many families, the cause of daily vexation, and of continual though fruitless complaints. We must receive with patience and good nature, numberless little failures in those whose happiness it is to think little of the effect they produce upon others; nor is it by reproofs and admonitions, showered down upon the child at the moment in which we wish him to display his good manners, that we shall effect our purpose; but by accustoming him to exercise habi-

12*

tual kindness and civility towards his companions, and those with whom he lives. With all our care, however, we are not to expect that the manners of children will be superior to those of the persons with whom they chiefly associate; for, in nothing is it more true that " we are all a sort of chameleons, and still take a tincture from things around us." On this account, as on every other, it is of importance that children should witness no vulgar habits in the nursery, and that the conversation between the nurses themselves should be guarded and correct.

But here it must be remarked, that in our earnestness to render our children pleasing, and to improve their manners, care will be required that we do not rob them of their chief charm, the simplicity of childhood; for how greatly are to be preferred, even an uncouthness of behaviour, and awkward shyness, to any thing of premature forwardness, formality or affectation!

" Affectation is but lighting up a candle to our defects, and though it has the laudable aim of pleasing, always misses it."* We must also avoid working upon vanity to secure good manners, lest we nurture that love of admiration which is apt, but too soon, to take an overbearing possession of the heart.

ORDER.—The general order of a nursery will be greatly promoted by early rising, by regular hours for all the employments of the day, and by an attention to this maxim,

" A place for every thing, and every thing in its place."

Method and true order are attainments of a higher stamp than is generally

* Locke.

supposed; for they are not only useful in the lesser concerns of life, but necessary to success in the most important objects: it is by these that the powers and activity of the mind are turned to good account. " Method," as Mrs. H. More says, " is the hinge of business, and there is no method without order and punctuality." " Method is important as it gains time; it is like packing things in a box; a good packer will get in half as much more than a bad one."*

* Cecil.

RELIGIOUS INSTRUCTION AND RELIGIOUS HABITS.

RELIGIOUS education has been so ably and satisfactorily treated in several works already before the public,* that the author would be unwilling, even were she competent, to offer a full or connected disquisition on the subject. But as she could not entirely omit that which is the foundation of all good education, she has slightly touched upon some points, which from her own experience she conceives to be of particular importance.

" The spirit of true religion is diffusive, and therefore, they that are actuated by it, as they wish the happiness of all, so they labour to set them in the right way that leads to it, and more especially will they do so, with respect to those

* Monro's Pious Institution of Youth—Babington's Practical View of Christian Education.— Doddridge's Sermons on Education; and the Works of Mrs. Trimmer, and Mrs. H. More, on the same subject.

whom the divine Providence has put under their *immediate* direction and conduct, whom the Father of spirits hath committed to their care as so many talents which he expects they should improve for his service and to his glory. Parents should remember that their children are designed to be citizens of another world, and therefore that their *principle* study must be how to fit them for the employs of that blessed state. The *instinct* of nature prompts parents to do good to their children; but *religion* exalts those instincts, gives them more noble tendencies, higher aims, and a diviner bias."*

It is the deeply-rooted conviction, that in bringing up a child we have to do with an immortal spirit, which can alone excite that strength of feeling, and depth of interest, essential to the performance of our highest duties toward him. That many well-meaning parents, who take it for granted they are bringing up their families religiously, manifest so little earnestness in the cause; that religion is, in fact, made so secondary an object, must in

* See Monro's Pious Institution of Youth, vol. i. pages 18, 19, 33.

many cases be attributed to the want of strong practical faith ; to the want of a real and operative belief in the solemn and repeated declarations of Scripture, that the present world is but a state of probation, and that on the short time spent here, depends the everlasting condition of every individual. Amidst the various cares, engagements, and pleasures of life, there is great danger of neglecting those things which though most important are least seen. We are called upon to apply ourselves in earnest, and " whilst it is culled to-day," to the religious improvement of our children, as those whose " time is short," as those who remember that in this case there is a double uncertainty, in the lives of their children, and in their own, as those who know that the present *may* be the *only* opportunity of performing the high duties required at their hands. But enlightened zeal is ever accompanied by wisdom and prudence—our efforts will many times be hidden and unseen, for when outward exertion would be ill-timed or injudicious, may not a parent promote the best interests of her children by that unobserved vigilance, that spirit of the heart, which we may confidently believe will not fail of its reward

Some parents are deficient in the religious care and instruction of their children, from the false notion, that as it is divine grace alone which can change the heart, so they have little else to do than to sit still, and leave their children to the operation of that grace; supposing that with it all will be well, and that, without it, whatever they can do is to little purpose: whilst others fall into the contrary extreme; and, confining their views to human efforts, often fail by imposing burthensome restraints, and rendering religious duties laborious and wearisome :—but there is a happy medium between those opposite errors.—The belief that God is pleased to work by means; that he has graciously promised to bless the faithful use of these means; that he has declared, as we sow, so also we shall reap ; that he has commanded us " to train up a child in the way he should go, and when he is old he will not depart from it ;" this belief will stimulate to a diligence, a constancy, and a fervency of spirit in the religious education of our children. At the same time, the sense of our own insufficiency—the conviction, that although we may plant and water, it is God alone who can give the increase, will combine that moderation with our earnestness and activity ; that calmness and quietness with our zeal, without which they will often prove ineffectual, and *should* lead us to implore the divine aid and blessing so graciously promised by those who ask.

13

It is not to be forgotten, that as religion is the most important, so also it is the most sacred of all subjects; and that although, from its importance, it is ever to be kept in view; yet, from its sacred character, it must not be made too common or familiar.

" True religion," (a late valuable writer remarks) " may be compared to a plum on the tree, covered with its bloom; men gather the plum, and handle it, and turn and twist it about, till it is deprived of all its native bloom and beauty." We are in danger of doing this, if we impart religious instruction as a task, either to ourselves or our pupils: if we attempt to teach the sacred truths of Christianity, whilst we have little sense of their beauty or of the savour that attends them; if we are in the habit of bringing forward religion without a corresponding feeling and reverence; if we can talk of it with the lips, whilst the heart is little alive to the subject; and if we imperceptibly adopt a religious tone, because it prevails amongst those about us. By this mode of proceeding, we may encourage in those under our influence an outward profession of what is good; but we are not likely to foster that substantial and practical principle, which is the life of religion.

It is a very mistaken idea, and not the result of experience, that regular connected teaching is unnecessary on religious subjects. We have the divine command, "thou shalt teach them diligently." It is therefore our absolute duty to obey, and to enlighten the understandings of our children in religious truth, in proportion as they are able to receive it. But we are to enter upon this work, not as we would undertake the dry routine of a common lesson, but as a business in which we peculiarly need that wisdom which cometh from above; as a business that has to do with the heart more than the head; in which our chief endeavour shall be to engage the inclination and affections of our pupils; a business of incalculable importance, as regarding the most momentous interests of those to whom we are bound by the tenderest ties. In the study of the Scriptures, it is not enough to read them as a letter, it should be our desire to imbibe ourselves, and to infuse by sympathy into the hearts of our children, a measure of that spirit which breathes throughout them. We would not, for example, give them the particulars of the life and death of the Lord Jesus, merely to be accurately learnt and remembered as any other subject of historical information; but it ought to be our object so to communicate this most interesting of all narratives, as to excite in their hearts a love and gratitude towards him as their divine and compassionate Redeemer.

Although we would not lessen the value of other means of instruction, it is evident that the most important and purest source of religious knowledge, is the simple, unprejudiced study of the Bible. If we take the Scriptures in their regular order, omitting only those parts which are above the comprehension of children, they will supply " that which is able to make them wise unto salvation :" every christian doctrine, every important precept will be presented in succession, and will afford the most favorable opportunity for useful observations and individual application; and these will be most likely to prove beneficial when they spring naturally from the subject before us, and from the lively feeling which it excites. Fenelon advises, that we should not only tell children that the Bible is interesting and de-

13*

lightful, but make them *feel* that it is
so. We should endeavour to make
them feel the deep interest of the narratives it contains, and the exquisite
beauties with which it abounds. This
cannot be accomplished if they read it
as a task; an historical acquaintance
with Scripture is, indeed, very desirable; but it is from a *taste* for, and an
interest in the sacred writings, that
the most important benefits are to be
derived.

As children are little capable of receiving abstract ideas, it is probable
that they will not derive much benefit
from being instructed in doctrines
separate from facts—by facts, we may
convey a strong and simple view of
the most important truths of Christianity. If, for example, we can represent in lively colours to their imagi-
nations, the beautiful history of our
Lord calming the storm when " the
waves beat into the ship," and his

voice was " mightier than the noise of many waters," they will imbibe a stronger and more practical sense of his Almighty power, than could have been imparted to them by any bare statement of his divinity. We shall also best be able to impress upon their minds his infinite mercy and compassion towards us, by reading or relating to them, so as to realize the transactions, and interest the feelings, such narratives as those of our Lord's taking the infants in his arms, and blessing them; of his raising the widow's son, of his healing the lunatic child, and lastly, of his suffering and dying for our sakes, that we might be made the heirs of eternal life.

It is of great importance that all religious instruction be given to children with reference to *practice*. If they are taught that God is their Creator and Preserver, it is that they may obey, love and adore Him; if that

Christ is their Almighty Saviour, it is
that they may love him, give themselves up to him, and trust in him alone
for forgiveness and salvation.   If, that
the Holy Spirit is the " Lord and
Giver of life," it is that they should beware of grieving that secret guide,
which will lead them out of evil, will
enable them to bring forth the fruits
of righteousness, and prepare them
for a state of blessedness hereafter.
The *omnipresence* of God should also
be strongly and practically impressed
upon the mind in early life, not only as
a truth peculiarly calculated to influence the conduct, but, as a continual
source of consolation and support in
trouble and danger.

It is to be remembered, that religious instruction is not to be forced
upon children: wisdom is required in
communicating it to them, that we
may give them food " convenient" for
them, nourishing them, not with strong

meat, but with " the sincere milk of the word," that they may grow thereby ; making the best use of the natural and gradual opening of their understandings ; and we may acknowledge, with thankfulness, that there is something in the human mind which answers to the most simple and sacred truths :——the mind of man seems formed to receive the idea of Him who gave it being. A *premature accuracy* of religious knowledge is not to be desired with children : but that the views of divine truth which they receive, should be sound and scriptural, and so communicated as to touch the conscience. If the conscience be touched ; if the fear of God be excited ; a fear to offend him ; a dread of sin ; there is something to work upon, and a foundation is laid for advancement in religion, as the character ripens. But we are not to forget the general balance of Scripture, or to give force to one part by overlooking another. Thus, in our endeavours to touch the conscience, and to excite a dread of sin, we must also be careful to represent our Creator as the God of love, the God of peace, the Father of mercies,—to direct the attention of our children to that "Lamb of God, which taketh away the sin of the world;" that the result of our labours may, with the divine blessing, be a union of fear and love in the hearts of our pupils; that tenderness of conscience should not lead to the spirit of bondage; nor fear degenerate into religious terror, and, consequently superstition.

In the minds of many people, from the want of this early judicious care, religion and superstition, quite unknown to themselves, have become strangely interwoven. They surrender themselves to superstitious or enthusiastic impressions, because they do not distinguish them from the voice of truth, and feelings of piety; but enlightened religion is, in fact, in direct opposition to superstition : they are as different as light from darkness ; for superstition quits the solid ground of revealed truth, and forms conceptions for itself, of what the Divine will may be towards his creatures. But it should be our object, to give to children a scriptural, and, therefore, a reasonable and healthful view of religion ; to guard them against all that is erroneous and morbid, and to prepare them for the reception of " the spirit of power, of love, and of a sound mind."

The curiosity so natural to children is not to be hastily repressed, on religious subjects ;—we are rather to direct than reprove it, remembering

that, within due bounds, the exercise
of the natural powers may be made
subservient to the most important
ends in acquiring religious knowledge.
At the same time, any tendency to a
critical, cavilling disposition, is to be
uniformly discouraged, nor is it of
small importance, that children should
be guarded against the influence of
those from whom they may imbibe
such a habit of mind.   As their understandings improve, they may be
led to consider the infinite distance
between God and man,—that " He is
the high and lofty One that inhabiteth
eternity," whilst man is like " a sha-
dow that declineth," or as the grass
of the field, which " in the morning
flourisheth and groweth up, but in the
evening is cut down and withereth ;"
that we see but as the smallest part
of the works of God ; and of that small
part, much is to us incomprehensible ;

—but that, great as he is, his love extends to the meanest of his creatures; that, for man he has provided eternal happiness; and that, in the Scriptures he has been pleased to reveal all that is necessary for us to know and believe, in order to attain it. That we are, therefore, to approach these treasures of heavenly knowledge, with no expectation of finding every difficulty solved, or all made clear to our weak and narrow understandings; but, with a humble and teachable disposition, for spiritual food, and for spiritual life: knowing that " the secret things belong unto the Lord our God; but those things which are revealed belong unto us and to our children for ever, that we may do " them. If we attempt to explain the deep mysteries of religion further than the Scripture has explained them, we shall be more likely to degrade what

14

is most sacred, and perplex the mind, than to enlighten the understanding, or elevate the affections.

RELIGIOUS HABITS.

BESIDES the religious instruction of children, we have also to attend to the formation of religious habits. If these be well established in early life, even though the heart be not always engaged in them as it ought to be, yet something is gained. Such habits frequently become the channels through which spiritual good is conveyed— besides, whenever the vital principle of religion begins to operate, they render the path of duty less difficult.

Amongst the most important religious habits may be ranked the daily exercises of devotion,—a fixed time and plan for reading the Scriptures; a regular attendance, and a serious behaviour, at a place of worship; and a practical regard to the Sabbath; and, if practicable, an attendance upon Sunday schools. The practical results of Sunday schools show them to be great nurseries of piety.

DEVOTIONAL EXERCISES.——In · bringing up children to regular and stated devotional exercises, it will be also necessary to instruct them in the true nature of prayer; and this may best be done by examples. We may remind them that the women of Canaan prayed, when, though often rejected, she still called upon her Saviour, "Lord, help me;"——that the disciples prayed, when, in the midst of the tempest, they cried, "Lord save us, we perish;" (Matt. viii.)——that the publican prayed, when he smote upon his breast, saying "God be merciful to me a sinner;"——that the blind man prayed, when, notwithstanding many discouragements, he still repeated, "Thou son of David, have mercy upon me;"——and that these are all instances of that fervent and humble prayer of the heart, " which availeth much."*

Children may be asked, if they were hungry or athirst, distressed or in danger, in what manner they would call upon their earthly parents for relief and deliverance; and reminded that it is with the like earnestness they should beseech their heavenly Father to pardon their sins, to strengthen their weakness, " to deliver them from evil," and to grant them his favour, which is better than life. Their attention should be directed to the powerful and tender affections of their earthly parents towards them; that from this consideration they may be the better able to comprehend the love of God, as being infinitely greater, more tender, and unchangeable. They

* See an excellent paper on Prayer, printed by Forbes, Brighton

14*

may be taught, that as God heareth the ravens cry, and satisfieth the wants of every living thing, much more is he ever attentive to the feeblest desire, or the least sigh raised in the hearts of his children toward him : that it is the prayer of the heart alone which is acceptable in his sight, although a form of sound words is valuable as an assistance in raising the affections, and confining the wandering thoughts.

But children are too often suffered to repeat their prayers with as little reflection, and almost as little reverence, as they manifest in the common engagements of the day. We should endeavour to bring them into a serious and tranquil state of mind before they kneel down. They may then be reminded of their faults with good effect, and thus gradually accustomed to unite self-examination with the duties of devotion; examination not only of their outward conduct, but of their motives; a habit so essential to real religious advancement !

The morning and evening afford the best opportunities for devotional exercises; and it should be our earnest desire to accustom our children to begin and close the day with Him in whom they "live, and move, and have their being;" to accustom them "to seek *first* the kingdom of God:" to make it their first business on waking to give thanks for the mercies which are "new every morning," and to seek for daily strength, support, and protection; that thus, when they rise, they may still be with him; that he may

"Guard their first springs of thought and will
  And with himself their spirits fill."

In the evening, when they have prayed for pardon and peace, let us endeavour to infuse the spirit of that beautiful expression in the Psalms,

" I will both lay me down in peace
and   sleep,   for   thou,   Lord,   only,
makest me dwell in safety." At no
time is the influence of a mother more
valuable than when her children are
retiring to rest.   It is then, that having
ceased   from   the   business   and   the
pleasures of the day, their minds are
quieted,   their   feelings   more   tender,
and   more   fitted   for   the   reception of
religious impressions.   Happy is it if
the spirit of her own heart be such as
to enable her to make full use of these
favoured   moments ;   to   make   use   of
them   as   valuable   opportunities   for
withdrawing   the   hearts   of   her   children from things which are temporal,
and   of   fixing   deeper   and   more   lively
impressions of those which are eternal.
In   the   absence   of   a   mother   on   these
occasions, it is the duty of an assistant   as   far   as   possible   to   supply   her
place.   When a child has repeated his
evening prayers, she should not allow.

him to return to trifling conversation
or common pursuits, but take him
quietly to bed, and she will find it
beneficial and gratifying to him then
to read a psalm or hymn, as the last
thing before she leaves him.

'The prayers of children should be
simple, and suitable to their understandings and state of mind: we must
not, however, expect that they will
always enter into them with the feeling we may desire. Yet, as we are
to persevere, through all discouragements, in the performance of this sacred duty ourselves, must we not also
train up our children to it, notwithstanding their great infirmities, in
simple obedience to the express commands of God; in humble reliance on
his blessed promises; and with full
confidence in Him who is not an high
priest that cannot be touched with
the feeling of our infirmities, but who
ever liveth to make intercession for

us ? and might we not hope, that the prayers of our children would be less defective, were the spirits of those about them more serious and more devotional ?

A love for the sublime and beautiful works of nature should be early cultivated, not merely as affording a source of pure enjoyment, but as a taste, which, if properly directed, may promote a devotional spirit, and elevate the mind, by raising the views, through " things which are seen," to Him who is invisible.

" Happy, who walks with him ! whom what he finds
   Of flavour, or of scent, in fruit or flower ;
   Or what he views of beautiful or grand
   In nature, from the broad majestic oak,
   To the green blade that twinkles in the sun,
   Prompts with remembrance of a present God !
   His presence, who made all so fair, perceived,
   Makes all still fairer."

GRACE BEFORE MEAT. —— Children should be taught to receive their daily bread as from the hand of God, and that excellent custom of grace before and after meat ought surely to be kept up in the nursery, as an open acknowledgment of gratitude to the Giver of all good.

DAILY STUDY OF THE SCRIPTURES.— It will be of advantage if the daily portion of scriptural instruction can be given to children as the first employment, after their morning prayers! and it is much to be desired that parents would retain this part of education in their own hands; for the situation of a parent gives advantages for the performance of this duty, which are rarely possessed in an equal degree by a tutor or governess. Perhaps the earliest scriptural lessons are best given in conversation, assisted by prints.* By this simple method,

* It is related in the life of Dr. Doddridge, prefixed to his Works, that " his parents brought him

even very young children, before they
can read, are capable of understanding, and of profiting by, many parts
of sacred history. - A reference to
Wallis' map of Canaan, with little
figures, and when children are old
enough, to Burden's Oriental Cus-
toms, or Calmet's Dictionary, will
add to the interest of the historical
parts of the Bible, and will contribute
to render the Scripture lessons amusing as well as instructive.

THE SABBATH.——As the common
business of life is to be laid aside on
the Sunday, so the engagements of
this day should be of a wholly different character from those of the week;

up in the early knowledge of religion. Before he
could read, his mother taught him the history of
the Old and New Testament, by the assistance of
some Dutch tiles in the chimney of the room where
they usually sat, and accompanied her instructions
with such wise and pious reflections as made strong
and lasting impressions upon his heart."

and if a practical regard to the Sabbath be early established, and its employments, which may so easily be done, are rendered attractive and interesting, children will enter upon them from choice, and neither expect nor wish for any others.

The study of the Scriptures may be agreeably diversified, either by looking out, with the assistance of marginal references and a concordance, the various texts on one particular subject, as, on prayer, almsgiving, duty to parents, &c.; or by tracing the chain of prophecy relating to the Messiah, with corresponding passages in the New Testament; by studying the types which beautifully illustrate his character and offices—as the paschal lamb—the brazen serpent—the scapegoat, &c.; or by reading, with a particular reference to the lives and characters of eminent individuals—as of Abraham, Joseph, Moses, David, &c.

15

The Liturgy, as well as the Catechism, will also afford an excellent groundwork for scriptural research; and there is no doubt but that the services of the Church might be rendered more benefiicial to children, if previously explained to them, and illustrated by those passages in the Bible from which they are derived. Nor is it necessary that children be confined, on the Sunday, to studying the Scriptures, Catechisms, &c.:—there are many books suitable to the day, which will afford an agreeable and useful variety, and which, if laid aside in the week, will be read with greater pleasure. Hymns, or a portion of Scripture,* may also be committed to memory: but care will be required that these be neither learnt as a common task, nor repeated in a hasty or irreverent manner. When children write with some facility, they

* See Mr. Babington's excellent remarks on this subject—Practical Essay, page 94, &c.

will derive pleasure from copying out hymns; select passages from the Bible; or the texts they have looked for, on particular subjects, in a book, kept for the purpose. They may, besides, be formed into a class, and questioned, on Sunday, in their Scriptural knowledge; and it will add to the interest, if the children of more than one family can be united in this exercise.

When old enough, they may be permitted to share in the labours of a Sunday school as teachers, or make choice of a poor child as a private scholar:—such objects are valuable, as affording suitable occupation for the Sunday; but still more so, as having the tendency to foster a spirit of active benevolence, and a disposition to promote the interests of others.

The engagements to which we have referred, with an attendance on public worship, and necessary recreation and exercise, will fill up the Sunday usefully and agreeably.   If we enter into the full meaning of these expressions— "shall call the Sabbath a delight, the holy of the Lord, honourable,"* we shall be persuaded, that it is not sufficient to enforce a strict regard to the Sabbath as a law; but that we should also endeavour to infuse a love for the day, as one of peculiar privileges; and parents may promote this feeling, by keeping in view that it is to be a time of rest, as well as of religious duty, by devoting themselves more than ordinarily to their children; and by rendering the Sunday the season for the best kind of domestic enjoyment.

PUBLIC WORSHIP.—Silence, self-subjection, and a serious deportment, both in † family and public worship, ought

* Isa. lviii. 13.

† It may not be irrelevant to the subject before us, to observe, not only the value of family worship *for the sake of our children*, but also the importance of conducting it, so as to render it to them a

to be strictly enforced in early life ; and it is better that children should not attend, till they are capable of behaving in a proper manner. But a practical respect for the Sabbath and for the services of religion, is but an effect of that reverence for *every thing sacred,* which, it is of primary importance early to establish as a *habit* of mind. No subject connected with religion ought to be treated lightly in the presence of children. If, for example, we think that we may employ the words of Scripture in a jocose or trifling manner, that we may make slighting remarks on the sermon of the day ; that we may ridicule the voice and manner of the preacher ; that we may speak con-

profitable and attractive service. "Let them find *it short, savoury, simple, plain, tender, heavenly.* Worship, thus conducted, is an engine of vast power in a family. *Family religion* is of unspeakable importance ; the spirit and tone of your house, the bye conversations in your family, will have great influence on your children."—(*Cecil's Remains.*)

15*

temptuously of others, because their
religious principles or habits differ from
our own, without injury to ourselves,
at least we are in danger of leading
our children to view religion through
a critical and satirical medium; and
thus to throw in their way one of the
greatest hindrances to religious advancement.   To take the name of God
in vain, (as, by using it in common
conversation, or on every emotion
of fear and surprise,) is an offence so
glaring, that a warning against it might
be unnecessary, were it not that some,
even well-meaning people, almost unknown to themselves, are apt to fall
into it, from the effect of example, and
early habit.   Such a use of the Divine
name, is not only to be most seriously
prohibited, but those exclamations,
which, in fact, convey nearly the same
meaning; as Mercy! Bless me! Good
Heavens! Good gracious! &c.

Firmness, and, sometimes, resolution and authority, may be required in the first establishment of religious habits; and, as far as it is necessary, they should be exercised; but never in such a manner as to render the most sacred duties a galling and burthensome yoke. An excess of strictness is injurious in the general management of children; but it is especially to be avoided in their religious education. If, in that, we draw the line too tight, we may not only excite a distaste for what is good; but induce concealment and hypocrisy. In religion, more than in any other object, it is of the first importance to gain over the affections; to draw the hearts of our children by the chords of love; that they may know, and feel for themselves, that " her ways are ways of pleasantness;" and that " all her paths are peace :"—

" Nor know we any thing so fair,'
As is the smile upon her face."*

Care must be taken not to press *too closely* upon children such non-essential points as form the distinguishing peculiarities of the various sects of Christians. It is a question worthy of much serious consideration, whether such points are of a nature to be imposed as a law upon those who are placed under our authority; and whether in doing this, there may not be a danger of " teaching for doctrines the commandments of men," and of fettering the conscience, by false associations of right and wrong? We are more likely to prepare our children for the reception of truth, if secondary distinctions are not brought into prominent view, and if our efforts are directed to the great object of leading them to that knowledge of God, and of his

* Wordsworth's Ode to Duty.

son Jesus Christ, which alone is life eternal.*

If children live under a religious influence, some vigilance will be required, lest they should assume a seriousness which is not real. Every thing unnatural, every thing bordering on hypocrisy, is to be most carefully checked; and that divine test deeply impressed on their hearts, as on our own—" If ye love me keep my commandments." We must not, therefore, force either the feelings or expression; satisfied, that if the true principles of Christianity have taken possession of the heart, it will necessarily manifest itself in something better than in words or profession.

Children must, besides, be guarded against placing too much dependence upon external observances. We are to bring them up with a reverence and a value for the ordinances of religion;

* John xvii. 3.

and to accustom them to a diligent and persevering attendance upon them as a sacred and important duty, to which secondary objects ought always to yield. But, at the same time, they will be able to understand that these ordinances, of themselves, are wholly insufficient; that he is a Christian " who is one inwardly ;" and that our real character is determined, not by that which we may appear before men, but, by that which we are in his sight, who " looketh on the heart."

CONCLUSION.

In concluding this little Work, the Author would, once again, remind all who are engaged in the care of children, that much patience and much perseverance will be required in the fulfilment of their duties toward them; and that they may hope to succeed, " not so much by the vehemence, as by the *constancy* of their exertions." We must not expect to witness the immediate fruit of our labour. The husbandman scatters his seed, " and hath *long* patience for it ;" and we are commanded, " in the morning to sow the seed, and in the evening to withhold not our hands : for we know not whether shall prosper."* To those who are conscientiously employed

* Eccles. xi. 6.

in the business of education, there is the most solid ground for encouragement : and it is of no small importance that they should cherish a hopeful and cheerful temper of mind. This will not only increase the vigour of their efforts, but greatly add to the probability of success.

Let us ever bear in mind the extensive benefit which may result from our bringing *one* child to choose and " hold fast that which is good." Have we not reason to hope that it will be a blessing, not only to himself, but to his children, and his children's children ? Does not the result of universal experience ; do not the records of history and biography, in addition to the express commands of Scripture, afford abundant encouragement for females diligently to exercise their powers in the education of children— powers which appear peculiarly given to fit them for the performance of this important duty ? How many eminent, how many excellent men have attributed their most valuable attainments to the impressions made on their minds by the early care of female relatives, and more especially by that of Mothers !

A Mother providentially possesses advantages for obtaining over her children an influence, which may be as powerful and durable, as it is mild and attractive; an influence, which may prove to them a guide and defence through the temptations and difficulties of life, when she, herself, has escaped from them all; and which, if it do not fully accomplish the good she desires, will yet " hang on the wheels of evil." It may confidently be believed, though she may have to wait " many days," that her conscientious endeavours will return in blessings upon herself, and upon her children ; and that the fruits,

16

whether earlier or later, will abundantly prove " that her labour has not been
in vain in the Lord."

APPENDIX.

MOTIVES THAT SHOULD INFLUENCE THE CONDUCT OF A NURSE.

WE are taught in the Scriptures (Coloss. iii. 23,) that, " whatever we do, we are to do it heartily, as to the Lord, and not unto men;" that " the eyes of the Lord is in every place, beholding the evil and the good;" (Prov. xv. 3;) and that " he will bring every work into judgment, with every secret thing, whether it be good, or whether it be evil." (Eccles. xii. 14.)

A real faith in these fundamental truths; a practical sense of the immediate presence of God, and of the unspeakable importance of our duty to him, alone can fit us to adorn the station in which we are placed, or enable us to render, at the last, a good account of our stewardship. Every other motive is variable, and comparatively weak; whether it be the desire of reputation and esteem, a sense of self-interest, or the dictates of natural affection. These may render us respectable in our outward conduct; they may produce some temporary good effects; but the foundation is wanting: the root is defective, and so will be the fruit. Religion alone can supply a principle, unchanging and unceasing: a principle which, depending not on the approbation of man, influences as powerfully in his absence as in his presence: a principle, that enables us still to go forward in the race set before us; "not weary in well-doing," but, for duty's sake, bearing trials and discouragements; surmounting difficulties, and overcoming temptations. When treating of the obligations belonging to any

station, it is to this principle they
must be referred ; and, in bringing
forward the particular duties of a
nurse, this it is which should be
strongly enforced as the original
source whence they must spring, and
without which, a nurse will do very
little, permanently, for the best interests either of children or of parents.
The standard of Scripture concerning
the duties of servants (as expressed in
Eph. vi. 5, &c.—Coloss. ii. 22, &c.—
1 Peter ii. 18, &c.) must be her rule
of conduct.

In undertaking the charge of a nursery, although such a situation afford
peculiar privileges, and peculiar satis-
faction, she will meet with difficulties in the discharge of her duty, much
to exercise her patience :—many an
anxious hour ;—many broken nights,
and wearisome days. And will she
not continually experience the need
of a higher motive than mere natural
16*

affection, or regard to worldly interest, to enable her to act with unvarying integrity toward the parents,
and with an uniformly right disposition toward the children,—such a
disposition as will lead to a constant
forbearance with them under their
little changes of temper and behaviour ; and, on all occasions, in sickness or health, by day or by night, to
the consideration of their real interest, rather than of any self-gratification.

Diligent attention to the bodily
safety and health of children, is a
duty of no small importance. In
this, a well principled nurse will consider herself peculiarly responsible,
and will feel that she cannot be too
watchful or assiduous : but she will,
at the same time, raise her views still
higher ; bearing in mind, that she is
also required, in dependence on the
Divine aid, to do all that is placed in

her power, to assist in training up
those under her care for everlasting
happiness. She will best promote so
invaluable an object by keeping her
own heart with all diligence, by her
example more than by precept and
advice; for " children better understand what they see and feel, than
the rules and reproofs which they
hear." In this view of the subject,
how highly important is the office of a
nurse! Little aware of it, perhaps,
herself, she is continually acting upon
" the first springs of character ;" her
children are hourly imbibing the spirit
that pervades her own mind. Much,
therefore, necessarily depends upon
her, but should this render her high-
minded or self-important ? Has she
not cause rather to suspect herself
and to fear always ? Knowing that in
proportion as her means of usefulness
are great ; so also is her responsibility
—so will be her criminality, if she

neglect or abuse the talents committed to her; and should not this consideration produce a desire to be instructed herself, and an humble deportment toward her superiors? Many valuable nurses are, in this point, eminently deficient; and their good qualities tarnished by a self-importance, and adherence to their own opinions, manifested even toward the Mother and her friends. Such a temper of mind, by inspiring the servant with undue confidence in her own judgment, independent of that of her mistress, is very unfavourable to the fixed determination which should actuate every nurse; to execute, as far as possible, the will of a Mother toward her children, when out of her sight; and *to be exactly the same to them in her absence as in her presence.* This is a law of primary and essential importance; a *directing principle* for the management of a nursery. If a nurse, on the unexpected appearance of her mistress experience a serious awkwardness—if she involuntarily change her manner or tone of voice, let her carefully examine if all is quite right, and set a stricter watch upon herself; let her inquire if she may not be blindly adopting wrong habits, because they are the common practice, and regulating her own conduct by the low standard of others.

"It is required in stewards that a man be found faithful." True fidelity regards not only the property of employers, but the *time*, the *care*, which are due to them; and such are the duties of a nurse, that they will not be faithfully performed, unless her *heart* be interested in their discharge. A servant who considers them a task, from which she is ever glad to be freed, in order to pursue other objects, is wholly unfit for her station. A conscientious nurse, therefore, will be cautious lest her own interests, pleasures, or even her sorrows, should so absorb the mind as to interfere with the performance of positive duties towards those committed to her care. Their welfare will be ever kept in view. She will be always unwilling to leave them, for any concern of her own, without the express consent of her mistress; and will never quit the nursery, if her mistress be out, for occasions on which this would not be allowed had she been at home. Such a nurse is not the lover of pleasure, but sober-minded, careful, and discreet. In her walks with the children, she will never carry them to any place or house which she was not sure would be approved by her mistress; she will avoid uniting with other servants and children: and at all times, will be cautious of entering into conversation with strangers; she will admit no visitors into the nursery, whom she would not wish her mistress to see there. Without her advice, she will be reluctant to give any medicine to the children, except in cases of absolute necessity; and would be shocked at the idea of administering a quieting draught, for the sake of her own ease (an offence which it is painful to acknowledge, has been too often committed) at the hazard of a dear child's safety! Nor will she attempt to sooth his fretfulness by bestowing upon him sweets or other indulgences, which might be injurious to his health. If her nights are disturbed by his restlessness, she will betray no temper or discontent towards her mistress, or yield to the least impatience toward the child. She will consider it her absolute duty to be equally diligent and affectionate in her attentions to him, however painful may be the effort of rousing herself when weary, and inwant of rest. It is melancholy to consider how many young children have fallen a sacrifice to the drowsiness and carelessness of their attendants; and, perhaps, no part of the business of a nurse calls for a greater exercise of good principle and self-denial, of tenderness and vigilance, than the care of a little infant by night.

The preceding examples are brought forward as instances of religious integrity; the necessary result of those principles which have before been stated as the foundation of all our relative duties.

Many nurses acting thus, are ornaments to society, and treasures to their employers; but that a number are influenced by motives far inferior, we have too much proof, not only in our nurseries, but also in the steets and public walks. Do not the showy dress; the flippant, vain, and flirting air; the manner evidently designed

to attract notice; the attention occu-
pied with self; the difference of de-
meanour in the presence and absence
of the mother; the rough handling,
and hasty words dispensed to their
little ones upon every slight offence :—
does not such a deportment bespeak
a mind unprepared for the important
duties of a nurse, and looking little
higher than to self-interest or pecunia-
ry recompense ?   It is not intended to
imply, that such servants are devoid of
natural affection to the objects of their
care, or that they would not be shocked
at the idea of doing them an injury;
but that natural affection alone will be
found wholly insufficient; and, when
undirected by principle and judgment,
will not exempt even the fondest nurse
from that selfishness, thoughtlessness,
and ill-temper, so highly injurious to
children.   The mere impulse of nature
will never produce a character essen-
tially valuable and useful. This must

be the result of religion, of self-denial,
diligence, and patience. Can any
stimulus to such conscientious efforts,
in the faithful discharge of our duties
to children, be greater, than to observe,
on every hand, individuals suffering
through life either in mind or body,
from the want of judgment, the defective principle, or the carelessness
of those who have brought them up?
such examples sufficiently prove, that
the well-being and happiness of children are permitted to be, in a great
measure, dependent upon the conduct
of those under whose care they are
placed. Shall we not, therefore, be
called to account for the use we have
made of the power which is thus given
us over others? And do we not need,
to direct us in the exercise of it, that
wisdom from above, which is first
" pure, then peaceable, gentle, and
easy to be entreated; full of mercy
and good fruits, without partiality and

without hypocrisy? Should we not also find it highly beneficial, to keep in view as a guide to our ignorance, the manner in which we ourselves are dealt with by our heavenly Father?— to bear in mind that the children intrusted to us, are not born under the rigours of the law, but under the merciful and fatherly discipline of the Gospel? He who set us the example that we should follow his steps, took the infants in his arms, put his hands upon them and blessed them, saying, " Suffer the little children to come unto me, and forbid them not, for of such is the kingdom of heaven;" (Mark x.) " He gathereth the lambs with his arm, and carrieth them in his bosom." (Isa. xl. 11.)—May not these beautiful passages be applied to the subject before us, as pathetically describing the love, the care, the compassion and tenderness required of us, and so greatly needed by the

helplessness, the dependence, the infirmities, and wrong tempers of childhood?

It is not impossible, that some who
are engaged in the care of children
may be discouraged by what has here
been insisted upon. They may be
tempted to say, "If these be the
duties incumbent upon us, how can
we be sufficient for them?" Let such,
however, remember that nothing un-
reasonable is required of them; that
they will have to render an account,
only in proportion to the talents committed to their trust. It is also encouraging to observe how often characters of small powers, under good
regulation, are rendered instruments
of great though inconspicuous usefulness. A young woman inexperienced,
and of moderate talents, may undertake a situation in a nursery: but if
she bring with her the foundation of
religious principle; a heart given up

to her employment; a sense of her own deficiency; and a wish to improve; there is every reason to expect, that, under good instruction, she will become a valuable servant.

We must all, indeed, in every situation, be prepared to fall short of that to which we desire to attain; but we are not to lower the standard of true excellence to our own imperfection. Rather should we, notwithstanding every discouragement, be constantly pressing towards the mark set before us; bearing in mind a just sense of the duties required of us, and performing them to the utmost of our ability. Then, whether this ability be less or greater, we have every reason to hope, that a blessing will attend our endeavours: for no uncommon powers; no extraordinary efforts; no new systems, are needed in the management of children; but the diligent, patient, persevering exercise of good principle, good temper, and ordinary good sense.

THE END.